# U.S.
# MILITARY
# POWER

# U.S. MILITARY POWER

## Steven L. Rys

Bison Books

Published by
Bison Books Corp.
17 Sherwood Place
Greenwich
CT 06830, USA.

ISBN 0 86124 129 0
Printed in Hong Kong

# CONTENTS

# INTRODUCTION

by William Koenig

The United States has always possessed great military power but for most of its history that power has been latent rather than actual. The colonial and early post-Revolutionary periods of American history were a time of high military threat and physical insecurity to which Americans had difficulty responding because the main element of their military power – men able to bear arms – was difficult to mobilize and sustain. Even so, the colonies could muster the resources to drive the Indians west of the Allegheny Mountains and stave off the British Empire long enough to win independence. And even without the participation of New England, Americans in the War of 1812 were again able to hold off the British Empire in what amounted to a second war for independence. Paradoxically, it was during this period of very real and often horrible physical threat that the historic American aversion to a standing military establishment was born.

With the conclusion of its second war with Britain, the United States emerged from its age of insecurity to face no immediate external threat in military terms until the early twentieth century. During this long period of 'free security', the United States was uniquely blessed, as a French ambassador noted, by weak neighbors to the north and south and to the east and west 'nothing but fish'. This blessing enabled the United States to function with essentially no military or foreign policy at all while its sources of latent military power – population, industry, agriculture, and technological knowhow – grew rapidly. Irrelevant to the development of the nation, only a miniscule standing military establishment was maintained. Never gathering in more than regimental strength for rare maneuvers, the army patrolled the frontier with up to half of its ranks composed of immigrants who had difficulty understanding orders in English. A small corps of engineers served a federal government whose largest component then was the postal service. And the few ships of the navy tried to look out for American commercial interests abroad. Only during the Civil War of the mid-nineteenth century was the vast potential of United States military power revealed in the population, industrial and logistics bases which could field mass armies and sustain them in the field for years while the economy of the North continued to expand.

When in the early twentieth century Americans began to perceive the existence of threats to their security abroad, they ended their century-long isolation through their first experiments with an active foreign and military policy. In a radical departure from American tradition, a mass army was committed to a coalition war in Europe in World War I and again in World War II. World War II is a great turning point in American history as for the first time military power was mobilized on a grand scale. So great were the resources and managerial capacity of the United States that it could fight two major but separate wars and still raise its standard of living appreciably.

The mobilization of its military power in World War II made the United States the most powerful nation in the world, the first global superpower, with its only rival the USSR, also immensely strengthened by its total mobilization in World War II. The development of United States military power in the postwar period has been influenced

The official seal of the US Department of Defense. The Department is the largest within the American political system. It was established by an Act of Congress in 1947 to take over the roles previously played by the Departments of the Army and Navy.

almost entirely by the growth of Soviet military power and American perceptions of the Soviet military and ideological threat.

That American security could be affected by factors beyond the continental United States was a truly revolutionary concept for Americans but was the basis for United States participation in the world wars and has been the basic principle of United States defense policy since then. Since World War II, the United States has maintained a large military deployment abroad in light of perceived security needs and twice has made major and costly military efforts in Asia. The United States has built an immense standing military establishment which presently absorbs over half of the national budget. These developments are directly counter to the historic American aversion to the standing military and peacetime military expenditure. They have been, however, accepted by the majority of Americans in the face of the military and ideological threat they perceive emanating from the communist world. Since World War II, military power has moved from the wings to centerstage in American life, often amid considerable controversy. Its adequacy and inadequacy (the 'how much is enough?' issue) have often been questioned as has its use (Korea, Vietnam and, most recent-

ly, Central America). It has been the center of presidential campaign rhetoric as in the 'missile gap' of 1960 and the 'ICBM vulnerability' issue of 1980. While the United States was indubitably the mightiest nation in history in the 1960s, Americans generally agreed that their military power had declined unacceptably, particularly vis-à-vis the USSR, in the 1970s and sent Ronald Reagan to the White House with some mandate to rectify the situation. Yet despite a fair consensus on the need for defense improvements, how that mandate should be fulfilled is the source of major controversy. Debate rages over the priorities of US military power, its role, and how much of the national treasure should be (or even can be) invested in its renovation. All agree on the magnitude and potential threat of the impressive Soviet military buildup over the last two decades but, as Steven Rys points out, actual war with the USSR paradoxically may be the least likely contingency US military power would have to face. In the years ahead, US defense policy and priorities face many complex choices and challenges as the US adjusts to a world in which it is no longer militarily supreme and where its national interests may be threatened in heretofore unexpected ways.

# AMERICAN NATIONAL INTERESTS

It is obvious that no country goes to the great expense of building and maintaining military forces without good reasons. The reasons, however, are confusing, contradictory, and very often obscure. American defense policy and military strategy are even more difficult to understand because of the complexity of nuclear doctrine and because many times the statements of government officials are less than totally honest. To understand better the American defense establishment of the 1980s (and the future), it is first necessary to understand how the present military doctrine was formed and the rationale, strategy, and weaponry behind it.

**Interests, Policy, and Strategy**

Almost every country in the world has some kind of security forces to protect its national interests whether these are as limited as Gabon's or as grand as China's. In general, America's and all other countries' national interests usually fall into one of three categories. First and foremost, every country's armed forces are designed to insure the bedrock national interest of survival. This means not only to insure the safety of its territory from attack and infringement, but in a broader sense to protect its way of life and culture. It includes the need to preserve and protect the govern-

ment and political system. Secondly, a country also has a national interest to insure its independence within the community of world nations. It seeks not only to determine its own foreign policy with other countries but also to be free to enter into trade and commerce. Anything less than the attainment of these two national interests means that the country is to some degree the satellite or surrogate of another, more powerful country. Thus defense policy must not only insure its territorial defense but also the wider defense of its rights to deal with other nations as an equal.

Finally, many countries have extended their national interests into a third ideological category. Such ideological national interests have often driven defense policy and military strategy in the past – the religious conquests of Spain in the New World and the wars that spread Islam both fall into this category. In the twentieth century one need only think of Fascism and Marxism/Leninism to recognise the influence of ideological national interest on defense policy. To be sure, more material national interests – economic or territorial gain – are often cloaked behind ideological motives for military action but the power of ideas is still there.

America has no official ideological national interests comparable to Marxism in the Soviet

Union. Many American political thinkers complain that the lack of a clear ideology has made it difficult for American administrations – to say nothing of our allies – to follow a consistent and effective foreign and defense policy. It would be a mistake, however, to believe that American leaders are not interested in regimes, alliances or causes friendly to the US and not only try to protect but also to foster such activities wherever and whenever possible.

No two country's national interests are exactly alike. Currently, America has very close political and military relations with many European governments. But the national interests of even the NATO allies sometimes sharply differ from those of the US, for example in the Middle East, causing considerable stress in the alliance. Moreover, national interests change with time and so do America's allies – both Germany and Britain have been deadly US enemies in the past. As countries grow richer or poorer, larger or smaller, so their national interests and therefore their defense policies and military strategies change. There is one and only one hard and fast rule concerning national interests and defense policy – a country never has permanent friends or permanent enemies.

Almost all American national interests are maintained or achieved in peace. When conflicts between American and other country's interests arise, they are often settled through negotiation and sometimes given to a third party for arbitration. The number of trade agreements and treaties signed every year by the US is a testament to the fact that most American goals are achieved peacefully. When results cannot be achieved peaceably, however, armed forces naturally assume the greatest importance. Lurking in the background of many negotiations involving the US is the realization by the other side that they are dealing with a superpower whose military capability extends to every part of the world and even into space. With some disputes, often concerning ideological interests, compromise is impossible. And in an era of nuclear weapons the need for a defense policy and strategy is more important than ever.

Defense policy, a term sometimes used interchangeably with defense doctrine, encompasses many aspects of a country's position on defense but, most importantly, it states the proposed objectives of its military forces in peace and war. In peace, defense policy should tell what kind of war is expected, how long it will last, and where it will probably be fought. Since 1945 United States' defense policy in peacetime has been almost as important as it has been in war, because in peacetime defense policy states how a country intends to use its forces if war should start. Thus with the forces and capabilities in existence, a peacetime defense policy can have the effect of stopping or deterring a war before it starts. During war, three defense policy objectives are possible. The first goal could be the

James Monroe, President 1817-25, whose Monroe Doctrine governed American foreign policy up to World War I, defined American national interests as being limited to the Western hemisphere.

complete destruction of the enemy armed forces, occupying his country, and eliminating his government – a total war with the goal of unconditional surrender. Second, the objective could be to drive the enemy's forces from a particular area claimed by both sides. Third, it may be to coerce an enemy to stop or start doing something; to force him to do what we want him to do.

Since World War II, American defense policy has followed all three of these goals with successes ranging from great to none in World War II, Korea and Vietnam. In war it is especially important that the goals of a defense policy be realistic and compatible with strategy so that the appropriate weapons can be used to achieve victory. In World War II the military aims of the US and its allies were explicit and the entire national effort was focused on achieving them. In Korea the goal was less clear ending with mixed but still acceptable results. The Vietnam War lacked clear realistic goals and was hindered by an impractical military strategy ending in defeat.

Strategy evolves from defense policy and deals directly with how the weapons will be used in war. Counterforce and countervalue nuclear strategies, against military and human and economic targets respectively, are means to the ends of defense policies of deterrence and warfighting. They state how the US will use its weapons in a nuclear war. Like defense policy the need for a practical strategy is evident not only in war but also in peace. Traditionally, strategy was almost the exclusive concern of

Top: Mexican troops storm the Alamo in 1836.

Above: General George Armstrong Custer, one of the youngest generals during the Civil War, later killed, (1876) at the Battle of the Little Big Horn.

Above right: General Ulysses S. Grant whose strategy of attrition based on industrial supremacy is only now becoming outmoded with the introduction of the Airland Battle scheme.

generals. In past wars goals would be set, the means provided by the governments, and military men would then be left largely alone to achieve victory. With the development of nuclear weapons, probably because of the monumental losses potentially involved, governments were no longer content to let military men alone determine strategy and civilian strategists began to exert a greater and greater influence not only on defense policy but also on the strategy employed to use weapons.

Although the relationship between national interests, defense policy, and strategy appear to be hierarchical, they actually interact and affect each other. As the fortunes of war wax and wane over time, some national interests may lose their value or others may appear. New weapons can change not only strategy and doctrine but may add an entirely new dimension to the meaning of national survival. The effect of nuclear weapons, for example, caused changes in all three areas of American national interests, policy and strategy.

## American Defense Policy and Military Strategy

It is somewhat ironic that for the first 170 years of its existence the United States had no real military policy or strategy. America did have national interests but these rarely caused the development of a defense policy. During wars the US government set goals and built military force to achieve victory. Afterward, the needs for a peacetime defense policy and strategy went unrecognized. To be sure, jingoistic Senators and Congressmen often threatened war, but the vast amount of this was rhetoric and was usually recognized as bluster by potential enemies because the US had no real capabilities to back up its threats.

Before 1945 the US did not maintain a large peacetime army because it did not need one. In line with the diplomatic policy of isolationism, America followed George Washington's warning to stay away from foreign entanglements and alliances and any chance of being involved in one of Europe's wars. Threats from Canada, after the war of 1812, and from Mexico were nonexistent. In many respects it is true that the US did not drive out major foreign powers from the hemisphere but bought them out with the Louisiana and later Alaska purchases. Because of the lack of a foreign military threat in peacetime, the US, unlike the countries of Europe, did not develop or appreciate the use of military strategy and policy in peacetime.

The Navy always fared better than the Army during the first century after America's independence. Most Presidents realized that while a standing army was not a necessity, a Navy – to protect American commerce and her shoreline – was needed to safeguard sea-related national interests. A Navy was also necessary to lend some credibility to the Monroe Doctrine. This bit of 19th century American hubris that warned all countries to stay out of the western hemisphere was about as close as the country came to a peacetime defense policy. In large measure it was a policy of weakness because the US depended in the early decades on the power of the British navy to keep any potential invaders out of the 'American' part of the world.

America fought a number of small, and one very large and bloody, wars during the 19th century. In many of these conflicts the goals of American defense policy seemed to be the enemy's unconditional surrender. Despite a number of limited military interventions south of the border, demonstrating the obvious utility of military force to achieve limited goals outside declared wars, American military tradition became fixed on the need to dictate terms to the enemy after his complete surrender. America waged a series of wars of attrition and annihilation over half a century against the Indian nations, gradually driving them back into reservations and opening up the West. American Marines fought their way to the Halls of Montezuma and dictated the peace terms to the Mexicans, adding a large section of land to the US. The Civil War ended not by negotiation, but by the complete economic ruin of the Confederacy, the fall of Richmond and Lee's surrender. While the US did not develop the tradition of having a

Above: The Civil War was one of the first conflicts to see widespread use of new means of transportation and equally extensive attempts by both sides to deny them to the enemy.

Left: The aftermath of a battle during the Civil War – the bloodiest of America's wars.

peacetime defense policy and strategy or an appreciation of military power in peacetime, the idea of the enemy's unconditional surrender and the occupation of his country took firm hold. This view caused considerable problems for American policymakers after World War II when more flexible policies were needed in pursuit of national interests through a defense policy and strategy whose real influence was felt in peace, not war.

The Spanish American War almost became the birthplace of modern American defense policy and strategic thought. For a time at least, the war caused American civilian and military leaders to expand their horizons beyond the narrow confines of continental US national interests. Through the ideology of 'manifest destiny' – the God-willed mission of America to democratize and civilize areas of the world – the United States expanded its territorial control to areas far from the US. In the end Americans rejected this 'destiny' and the empire died within a few years of its foundation. Following the Spanish American war the US again retreated into isolationism. While the Navy was kept relatively strong, the Army was allowed to deteriorate into little more than a cadre force of 80,000 men.

The battleship USS *Kentucky*, one of the ships of the Great White Fleet which made their famous round-the-world cruise in 1907-9, marking the United States' rise to the status of a world power.

Because of the Spanish American War, however, Americans had the opportunity to learn the lesson that military policy and power can help achieve goals beyond the basic defense of territorial boundaries. Through the influence of America's only great strategic thinker of the 19th century, Alfred Thayer Mahan, the US Navy expanded and modernized, and by the 1890s was able to play the key role in the battles for Cuba and the Phillipines. With these victories Americans began to see that not only could the oceans be used as a way for a fleet to prevent direct attack on the US but they could also be a means by which a powerful US Navy might travel thousands of miles to assure and protect American national interests in peace and war. Mahan stressed the importance of sea power as the key to any nation's acceptance as a world power. His ideas had a great influence on a young Assistant Secretary of the Navy, Theodore Roosevelt, who helped push an expanded naval construction program. While the US still did not develop a defense policy under President Roosevelt, TR's advice to 'speak softly and carry a big stick' got close.

When World War I erupted America had no real defense policy except to try and stay out of the conflict. This plan was successful for three

Teddy Roosevelt leads his Rough Riders in a charge during the Spanish-American War. Roosevelt became a national hero and later, as president, he helped develop a more active American foreign policy.

years. But while the US steadfastly refused to take part in the entangling alliances and politics of the Old World, the powers of Europe recognized the growing potential of the US. Germany and Great Britain both tried to get the US to join their side or plotted to involve the US in a diversionary war with Mexico. A reluctant President Wilson was forced eventually to abandon neutrality because of growing German attacks on American ships on the high seas. Lacking a clear defense policy of its own before the war, it is not surprising that when the US entered the war in 1917, it had no real strategy or idea of how to win the conflict. Although the presentation of the Fourteen Point Peace program was an admirable, if unrealistic, attempt to reconstruct the postwar world, Wilson and General Pershing, had no plans for the conduct of the war itself other than the defeat of Germany. Instead of trying to develop its own ideas, the US in large part adopted the Allied strategy of attrition. Luckily, the Germans were nearly exhausted by the time US forces arrived and the American Army was not subjected to the annihilating frontal assaults that killed hundreds of thousands of British and French soldiers at the Somme and Ypres.

Despite Wilson's postwar efforts to drag the US into the League of Nations, and provide some forum other than the battlefield to settle disputes, America relapsed into an isolationist posture again. The Army was demobilized. Americans, watching the postwar rush of the Allied powers for the spoils of war, again be-

Right: An officer and sergeant of the US Army in France in World War I.

came determined to distance themselves from Europe and its troubles. While no large peacetime military force was maintained, an increasing understanding of the role of potential American military power and the need and use of a defense policy was dawning. Official American postwar policy was to avoid future involvement, but American military planners drew up contingency plans for war against Japan, Britain and Germany among other countries. US military men took an avid interest in new weaponry and were among the innovators and developers of new systems and tactics. American naval officers examined the potential of the submarine and the US was among the first countries to recognize the importance of the aircraft carrier. American negotiators played a major role in the Washington Naval Conference in the 1920s which, for a time, established battleship building limits that influenced the strategy and defense policies of all of the world's great naval powers.

By the late 1930s the increasing military threat from Japan and Germany was growing more apparent to some American officials and after the Anti-Comintern Pact was agreed in 1936, plans for war against the two countries were begun in earnest. The sentiment among the vast majority of American people, however, was still profoundly isolationist and a defense policy advocating even minimal preparation to meet the Axis military threat and protect American national interests was politically dangerous. It was only through the skillful manipulation of public opinion that President Roosevelt was able to begin to help the British secretly and then more openly aid their war effort later on with Lend Lease.

With the bombing of Pearl Harbor in December 1941, all of America's national interests were threatened making the development of a successful defense policy and strategy the main focus of the entire war effort. As in World War I, America joined the conflict long after it started.

Below: President Wilson, second from right, leads a Liberty Loan fund-raising parade during World War I.

Bottom: Battleships of the US Navy are cheered by officers and men of the British flagship *Queen Elizabeth* on the American ships' arrival to join the British Grand Fleet at Scapa Flow, 7 December 1917.

mans into a two front war. In efforts to weaken the Germans, raise Allied morale, and lessen pressure on the United Kingdom, secondary invasions against North Africa and southern Europe were later launched when it was clear that the massive landing in France could not be launched quickly. A key aspect of the US and British strategy was the use of long range day and night bombing attacks on Germany and German occupied territory in Europe.

The Pacific war was not ignored although the defeat of Imperial Japan came second to that of Nazi Germany. In part this was due to the realization by all Allied planners that Tokyo's defeat depended on the control of the seas and a new Navy. Toward that end the US devised a

Top: American gunners bombard the German positions near St Mihiel in September 1918. Much of the equipment used by the US Army in World War I was, like this French 75mm gun, of foreign design – a token of American unpreparedness.

Above: An American ammunition column struggles up Beaumont Ridge, near St Mihiel, 15 September 1918. Although American combat troops quickly learned the lessons of trench warfare, the supply services were less efficient.

Once again, the US Army was small and had to be built up although some preparations for the draft had been made prior to the conflict. The attack on Pearl Harbor had dealt the US Navy a serious blow and reduced operations in the Pacific. Despite these weaknesses, the US did not accept the plans already made by the other Allies and instead took a leading role in planning strategy on how and where the war would be fought and won.

In a series of meetings between the American and British military commands, topped off with the conference between Roosevelt and Churchill in the early part of the war, a grand Allied military strategy to defeat Germany first and then Japan was formed. Although the Japanese bombed Pearl Harbor and forced Germany, to declare war on America Hitler clearly presented the greatest threat in 1942 and it was determined that the defeat of the Nazis was paramount. As part of the strategy of that defense policy, the US and Britain promised Stalin they would launch a second front in Western Europe as soon as possible. This would relieve pressure on the Soviet Union and force the Ger-

strategy based on island hopping. The plan called for Allied forces to gain gradual control of the sea leading to the Japanese mainland so that a force could be assembled close enough to Japan for an invasion. As with Germany, strategic air power was given an important role to reduce Japan's war making capability.

Although delayed repeatedly, the second front against Germany was eventually launched with the landing in Normandy in June 1944. Together with the Soviet advance into Eastern Europe, the end of Hitler's Thousand Year Reich was assured. The defeat of Japanese naval forces in key battles such as Midway, Leyte, and the Coral Sea, tightened American control over the Pacific. After fierce battles to retake islands, American forces reached Iwo Jima by early 1945 and bombers began to unleash terror on Japanese cities. Yet it was actually the American submarine blockade that brought Japan's war machine to a halt by late 1944 and virtually isolated Tokyo from its forces on the Asian mainland. American military planners prepared for the invasion of Japan which they predicted would be long and bloody, costing millions of Japanese and American casualties. But a historic event in the New Mexico desert, repeated on the Japanese cities of Hiroshima and Nagasaki, brought the war to a quick end.

While the atomic bomb ended the war it was actually the beginning of a new and unprecedented era for America. The US became the world's first military superpower. Most Americans did not immediately comprehend the true power of the atomic bomb and there were few in government who realized that the US would now be forced into a position of world leadership. In fact after the war the US was without question the preeminent power in the world. This was true not only because of its atomic power, but because it had emerged from the war much stronger than it had been in 1941. Britain and France were ruined after years of combat, their economies faltering or their political system threatened by assault from the communist dominated left. China, a victor in World War II, was locked in another round of civil war. Only the Soviet Union appeared to have the capability of challenging the US for world leadership.

It was not long after the war in Europe ended, probably at the Potsdam Conference, when the first chill of the coming Cold War was felt. American confrontations with the USSR over the next five years became increasingly tense as the Iron Curtain descended over Eastern Europe with crises in Berlin and Czechoslovakia, and later with the fall of China. While the UN could settle some minor disputes, it soon became clear that America needed a postwar defense policy and strategy in order to safeguard its interests. The development of a peacetime military strategy was unprecedented in American military history. Isolationism was truly gone forever.

During the period from the end of the war to 1949, and perhaps somewhat beyond, American defense policy was based on the atomic monopoly. The US had sole possession of a weapon of immense power – so powerful that many people mistakenly believed that it made all wars impossible and other kinds of military force unnecessary. Gradually, US government policy came to rely implicitly on the myth that atomic weapons were all powerful and could settle or thwart any problem. But Washington actually had to rely on nuclear power as the keystone of its military policy, for with the end of the war the American Army had undergone a rapid demobilization declining from 12 million to under two million men in less than a year. Although many military men, like General George C. Marshall, realized that such massive conventional disarmament forced a dangerous reliance on nuclear weapons, they were powerless to stop it. In 1945 Americans had had enough of wars, wanted to bring the boys home, and had no interest in keeping a large army in the US or abroad.

US defense policy throughout the Truman era in the late 1940s, was based on the threatened use of nuclear weapons against any Soviet attack on Western Europe. Stalin was thought to have maintained a multi-million man army in Eastern Europe to intimidate the West. If war came, this Russian steam roller would smash its way to the English Channel. During the Berlin Blockade Truman flexed American nuclear muscle and showed Washington's resolve to use it by transferring a squadron of B-29 bombers, capable of carrying atomic weapons, to bases in England from where they could reach cities in the Soviet Union.

As a result of this defense policy, the American Army and Navy were not revitalized even during the darkest days of the Cold War in the

late 1940s. Because of the reliance on nuclear weapons and the importance of strategic airpower, the new US Air Force gained great stature and played the central role in American defense policy for years to come. Some recognition of the need for more conventional forces to defend Western Europe was evident early in April 1949 with the formation of the North Atlantic Treaty Organization, NATO, but the dependence on nuclear weapons as the keystone of American defense policy and strategy remained.

Two events cast serious doubt on the Truman defense policy and strategy. In October 1949 an American plane taking air samples over the Pacific brought back evidence that the Soviets had detonated an atomic weapon. The American atomic monopoly was no more. The shock of this event on US policy makers, who had expected the Soviets to get the bomb someday but not that quickly, was terrific. Soviet possession of the bomb meant that the US and her allies would now have to face the fact that nuclear strikes and horrendous destruction would not be limited to one side. It meant that the Amer-

President Franklin Roosevelt and the industrialist Henry Kaiser examine a model of an escort carrier of the type then, 1943, under construction in Kaiser's shipyards. Industrial power was the foundation of America's success in World War II.

Bottom right: A P-51 Mustang, in many respects the outstanding fighter aircraft of World War II, in flight over England.

Main picture: The battleship USS *Missouri* at anchor in 1944. The *Missouri* and her sisters served in the later battles of the Pacific War and three of the *Iowa* class, including *Missouri*, are now being modernized to serve once again, this time as cruise missile carriers.

Right: The US Chiefs of Staff during World War II. From left, General Arnold, Army Air Force, Admiral Leahy, Chief of Staff to President Roosevelt, Admiral King, US Navy, and General Marshall, US Army.

ican strategy of a nuclear response to a Soviet attack on Europe was less and less believable since Moscow might now strike the US in return.

The second shock to the prevailing faith in the omnipotence of nuclear weapons was the invasion of South Korea in 1950. Now that the Soviet bomb effectively cancelled the US threat of a retaliatory strike, the chances of a conventional war actually increased. It became clear to many that America needed strong conventional forces for situations where Washington did not want to escalate to nuclear conflict. The US could have used its nuclear arsenal, as it threatened, in Korea but instead decided once again to build up its conventional forces and drive the enemy back. After over two years of conventional stalemate an armistice was eventually reached. Although Eisenhower threatened the Chinese with nuclear attacks, this action probably did not have much influence on the war since the real power behind the communist aggression against South Korea

Above: Fire-fighting operations on the deck of the carrier *Saratoga* after she had been hit by kamikazes off Iwo Jima in 1945. The US Navy's experience in carrier operations in World War II and to the present day gives it a unique world-wide capability.

Right: A tank destroyer of a Fifth Army unit fires on a German position in the Gothic Line in Italy in 1945.

was the Soviet Union which was no longer in the shadow of a US nuclear monopoly.

Unfortunately, the lesson of Korea – the need for a balanced defense policy with strong nuclear and strong conventional forces – was ignored after the war. Eisenhower feared the high costs of a defense budget with the massive sums necessary to build and keep large conventional forces. Instead his administration prop-

osed a defense policy based on a 'New Look' which was nothing more than a continued reliance on nuclear weapons. According to Ike's defense plans, US technology would provide a cheap long term nuclear deterrent. Now that the Soviets had nuclear weapons, the US would not rely on strategic nuclear weapons alone. The Eisenhower Administration placed increased emphasis on the development of tactical nuclear weapons. These weapons would be used in Europe in order to balance any conventional force difference between NATO and Warsaw Pact forces and, Ike hoped, still keep the war limited to Europe. In other attempts to bolster defenses around the USSR without the high costs of massive conventional forces, the Administration promoted a series of defense treaties – SEATO, CENTO, ANZUS – designed to throw a ring of alliances around the USSR and contain Moscow's imperialist activities.

The problems of the Eisenhower defense policies became evident very early, especially when they were carried to the extremes by Ike's Secretary of State, John Foster Dulles. It was Dulles who promoted the strategy of Massive Retaliation and went on to advance the US nuclear commitment to dangerous limits by threatening to unleash nuclear strikes on the USSR not only for attacks on the US or its allies but if the Soviet Union were to attack any other

US troops come ashore at Salerno, Italy, in September 1943. The landings at Salerno were among the most bitterly contested of World War II.

part of the world. He asserted that by making the Soviets see that the punishment for aggression in any part of the world would far outweigh the benefits, Moscow would be deterred. The key factor involved in such a confrontation with the Kremlin was, according to Dulles, a question of American resolve – a clear understanding by Moscow that the US would really go to the brink and use nuclear weapons. The American defense policy of Massive Retaliation was, therefore, supplemented with a 'strategy' known as 'brinksmanship'.

Critics quickly pointed out that in an era of two nuclear powers the defense policy of Mas-

Left: The placard on the truck proclaims the arrival of the millionth ton of Marshall aid for Greece, a photograph taken in December 1949. The Marshall Plan for aid to European countries was part of the so-called Truman Doctrine designed to create strong economies and control the spread of communism.

Below: US Air Force transport planes during the Berlin Blockade, when the Western-controlled sectors of Berlin were cut off from all other forms of supply by the Soviets.

Left: President-elect Eisenhower with men of the 3rd Infantry Division during his December 1952 visit to Korea.

Bottom left: Infantrymen of the 27th Division in trenches near Heartbreak Ridge, 10 August 1952.

sive Retaliation and especially the strategy of brinksmanship was a formula for either massive mutual nuclear suicide or US surrender and acquiescence. Washington could not expect the Soviets to believe that American bombers would attack over some small conflict far from either the United States or the NATO countries. Dulles' ideas were actually harmful because they put the US in a strategic corner. Without sufficient conventional forces to respond to a small war, the US would be forced either to launch an all-out nuclear attack on the USSR (and in turn probably suffer a Soviet attack) or watch passively without being able to do anything. If anything, brinksmanship reduced rather than raised American military credibility with the European NATO allies and the rest of the free world.

Dulles' policies were undermined even further by a new and unexpected Soviet capability to deliver strategic nuclear weaponry. In 1957 the USSR launched Sputnik and Krushchev made public boasts that the missile that launched the satellite could just as easily carry a nuclear warhead intercontinental distances. More importantly, the Soviets could also use their missiles to destroy US bombers on the ground thus carrying out an effective 'counterforce' attack eliminating America's nuclear deterrent.

John Kennedy came to the White House in 1961 determined to find a defense policy that would eliminate the weaknesses of Eisenhower's Massive Retaliation, especially in the face of Soviet missile advances, and leave the US with more military options than a choice be-

Below: Pershing M26 tanks fire on North Korean positions near the Naktong River in August 1950. The belief that all communist regimes throughout the world were directed in all their acts from Moscow was one of the motivations for the US involvement in Korea and was at the heart of American strategic thinking throughout the massive retaliation years and up to the time of the involvement in Vietnam.

Above: Vice President Nixon in debate with Soviet leader Nikita Kruschev in 1959. Kruschev's unjustified boasts of Soviet progress in rocketry helped create the 'missile gap' issue and played a part in forming American strategic policy in the early 1960s.

Right: Secretary of Defense McNamara arrives in London in 1962 for talks on the future of the British strategic nuclear forces. The British independent nuclear deterrent was later maintained by the purchase, at a bargain price, of Polaris missiles.

strike. If the US could preserve a deterrent force that would achieve these levels in a second strike, destruction of the USSR would be 'assured' and Moscow would be deterred from any thought of attack in the first place. This led to the Kennedy era nuclear strategy of Assured Destruction.

The Kennedy Administration also made significant changes with the build up of conventional forces. In the early 1960s the US began to rebuild the ground forces necessary to fight wars on less than a nuclear basis. Kennedy wanted a 'Flexible Response' that would allow the US to fight in Europe, or other areas, and not have to resort immediately to use of strategic or even tactical nuclear weapons for victory. The US would respond with forces appropriate to the level of aggression and try to avoid escalation to strategic nuclear holocaust. During the Kennedy and Johnson years, the US had the goal of building up conventional strength so that the US could fight 2½ wars at once; a major war in Europe, a major war in Asia, and a smaller 'brushfire' war somewhere else in the world. Through Flexible Response America's defense commitments would gain additional credibility because, while the Kremlin might gamble that the US would not risk escalation to strategic nuclear war over Europe, Washington's conventional defense capabilities and commitment to NATO would now be much stronger, more convincing, and hopefully more deterring to any kind of Soviet aggression.

The results of Kennedy's defense policy of Assured Destruction and Flexible Response had mixed effects. The strategic build up of US nuclear forces during the early sixties played a major role in forcing the Soviets to back down and remove their missiles from Cuba in October 1962. In fact, American strategic nuclear power increased so much in qualitative and quantitative terms that America reversed any previous vulnerability to the USSR and now actually had the capability to make a successful counterforce strike against Soviet forces, eliminating their deterrent. On the conventional side, Flexible Response may have led to a misapplication of force and a mistaken commitment. The build up of conventional arms, with the explicit goal of being able to fight the communists in less than a nuclear conflict probably made it easier for the Kennedy and Johnson Administrations to become involved in Vietnam.

The growth of America's nuclear arsenal in the early 1960s led to the development and proposal of other nuclear strategies which were not based on countervalue targeting or second strike deterrence. Defense Secretary McNamara proposed a 'no cities' strategy in 1962 designed to limit damage to either side's population by directing attacks only at each other's nuclear delivery systems. This plan raised alarm both in the US and abroad that America had embarked on a counterforce strategy and might choose to launch a disarming first strike

tween surrender and holocaust. On nuclear strategy Kennedy ordered that the nuclear deterrent be strengthened so that American retaliatory forces could unquestionably survive any Soviet first strike. Pursuit of this goal led to a speed up in the deployment and protection of the delivery systems of a triad of weapons – land based missiles, bombers, and missile firing submarines – each of which had offensive or defensive characteristics complementing the other. Kennedy's Defense Secretary, Robert S. McNamara determined that the destruction of 25-30 percent of the USSR population and two thirds of its industrial strength would be enough to deter any Soviet counterforce first on the USSR. McNamara was forced to back away from 'no cities', but the specter and advantages of counterforce remained and were to appear again as an explanation of both Soviet and US weapons in the coming years particularly during the Nixon and especially the Reagan Administrations.

With the exception of the brief appearance of McNamara's 'no cities' plan, American defense policy remained linked to retaliation and a strategy based on maintaining a secure deterrent capability throughout the Johnson Administration. According to certain American nuclear strategists, both sides had a secure second strike force which the other side could not destroy in a first strike, leading to a balance of terror which neither side could nor should want to upset. This policy later became known in-

famously as Mutual Assured Destruction or MAD. But MAD only 'worked' if both sides accepted it and did not try to upset the delicate balance.

In the late 1960s many civilian strategists and military men in Washington began to warn that the Soviets might not be playing by the rules – accepting the restraints of MAD – and were trying for something more. After the Cuban Missile Crisis the Soviets began their own massive strategic arms buildup – deploying over 1000 ICBMS over the next decade. At first many Westerners believed that this expansion was merely Moscow's attempt to gain equality or parity in nuclear forces with the US after the humiliation of October 1962. However as the number of Soviet delivery systems continued to grow in quantity and quality beyond

President-elect John F. Kennedy confers with President Eisenhower in December 1960. The flexible response strategy established by the Kennedy Administration holds good, in its main essentials, to the present day.

Inset, opposite: Men of the 1st Cavalry Division run from their UH-1D transport helicopter during Operation White Wing, near Bong Song, Vietnam, 19 February 1966.

Main picture: A C-47 transport plane explodes after being hit by a Viet Cong rocket during an attack on a Vietnamese air base in 1966.

A UH-1B helicopter gunship of the 1st Cavalry Division begins an attack run during fighting near Binh Dinh in 1967. Operations in Vietnam confirmed the vital role helicopters will play in any future conflict.

what was needed for a reasonably secure second strike, the fear of a possible Soviet counterforce capability grew even more.

But for most of the 1960s and the early 1970s the US was preoccupied with the war in Vietnam. That war is perhaps the best example of what happens when wartime policy, the objectives of war, are not matched by an adequate strategy, or means, to achieve the goal. Although the general war aim, to force the North Vietnamese to cease supporting subversion directly and indirectly in the South, was more or less clear, the military means to achieve this end were never allocated. Those means would probably have included the invasion and occupation of North Vietnam and the risk of war with China – a price that US leaders were not willing to pay. But because only limited means were provided, the political leadership, and more importantly, the country at large, should

have recognized that the aims would also be limited or unachieved. The incompatibility of wartime policy with strategy in Vietnam led to inconclusive results, frustration on the battlefield, disenchantment with the seemingly endless war at home, and eventually forced the US to pull out in the early 1970s. The effects of the lost crusade in Vietnam continued to haunt US defense efforts throughout the 1970s.

Much of the money and attention that could have been used to improve the American strategic nuclear deterrent or other conventional forces went into Southeast Asia. As a result, the capability of American forces in NATO declined, especially in the face of a large scale Warsaw Pact built up. By the late 1960s US military planners perceived the need to begin new programs to offset possible Soviet gains in the future by deploying an equal number of strategic nuclear systems to keep pace with the

Soviets or deploying a ballistic missile defense system to defend against the Soviet threat. Either way Mutual Assured Destruction had to be preserved.

Other voices within the Johnson Administration argued that it was pointless to begin another expensive round of the arms race. The Soviets would see any new US programs as an attempt by Washington to regain strategic superiority and the ability to coerce Moscow through a position of strength. The Kremlin would then build and deploy even more weapons with the end result that neither side would be more secure and hundred of billions of rubles and dollars would be wasted. To maintain Mutual Assured Destruction, the USSR and US should begin negotiations to limit strategic arms. Similar talks could also begin to limit the growth and potential threat of Warsaw Pact and NATO forces in Europe. The recommendations eventually led to the Mutual, Balanced Force Reduction talks in Europe, and the Strategic Arms Limitation Talks. The MBFR talks have never resulted in any reductions in Europe be-

Above: Vietnamese troops present arms for President Diem shortly before his assassination in 1963. Diem's government was notably corrupt and did little to stem the rise of the communist forces in South Vietnam despite the ever-increasing flow of American aid which he received.

Left: Fire is directed on a suspected Viet Cong position from a US Navy landing craft operating in the Mekong Delta in 1967.

cause of the problems of comparing different forces in different areas of the world but talks on strategic arms resulted in a dramatic, unprecedented treaty.

After four years of hard negotiations the SALT Treaty was signed in 1972. It was hailed as a major diplomatic milestone that preserved both sides' nuclear deterrent and began an era of detente. Under SALT I both sides agreed to deploy only a limited, small ABM system and to limit the number of their strategic delivery systems. SALT I was only supposed to be an interim agreement limiting arms and was to be followed by more comprehensive agreements

which would actually reduce the number of missiles on both sides. The treaty was seriously flawed, however, because it did not stop either side from continuing major research and development efforts to improve delivery systems. During the mid 1970s both sides took advantage of this loophole which threatened to undermine the nuclear balance as the accuracy of missile systems was gradually increased.

By the time the SALT II treaty was signed by President Carter in 1976, the winds of another cold war – Cold War Two – were already blowing. Soviet activities in Africa, Latin America and other areas were held up by critics as examples of how Moscow was taking advantage of a detente which had been too much in the Kremlin's favor. With the invasion of Afghanistan in December 1979 the SALT II treaty was withdrawn from Senate consideration although both sides have informally continued to abide by many of its provisions and limitations.

With the advent of the Reagan Administration to Washington in 1981, the US began another military build up comparable in scope to the early years of the Kennedy Administration 20 years before. American defense policy continued to be based on Mutual Assured Destruction and strong conventional forces but, as voiced by the President, there was a feeling on the American side that the Soviets had a definite superiority over the US. Toward redressing the strategic balance, this time in America's favor, Reagan's experts, led by Secretary of Defense Caspar Weinberger, increased defense expenditures in real terms to fund a wide range of programs. The area which caught the most public notice was strategic weaponry where the Administration, despite calls at home and abroad for a nuclear freeze, pushed ahead with new weapons systems, such as the MX missile, Trident submarines, cruise missiles, and resurrected the B-1 strategic bomber. Another area of particular attention was Europe and the need to increase both conventional and tactical nuclear

capabilities. In order to reduce criticism at home and especially in Europe the President balanced the military build up with calls for new Strategic Arms Reduction Talks (START) and a reduction or elimination of nuclear weapons in Europe.

**Future Policy and Strategy**
Future American defense policy and strategy will continue to be faced with the same hard choices in two areas – conventional and nuclear weaponry – that have been apparent since the end of World War II. How best with a large though limited budget, beset by other social needs at home, can the US meet its national security interests abroad? If American interests were only limited to the continental shores – if the US should again retreat into a new isolationism and abandon its commitments to Asia and Europe – its defense policy would become simpler and much cheaper. But American global interests have grown in the last 30 years, not decreased. The need to provide a reliable defense for North America and allies overseas has and will become even more important, complex, and costly.

Successful negotiations on the reduction of conventional forces in Europe are possible but even if they should bear fruit it is likely that the US will have to maintain large conventional

A dejected Marine waits to be evacuated from Con Thieu in 1967.

Left: Members of a long range patrol team establish a fire position. The establishment of the long range patrol groups was one of many attempts made by the Army to come to terms with the problems of jungle warfare.

Below: An anti-war demonstration. Opposition to the Vietnam War and the way the draft system operated led to the establishment of the all-volunteer forces.

A vital part of the United States' world-wide power projection capability is supplied by the attack carriers of the US Navy. Here an A-7E Corsair is seen in flight above the USS *America*.

forces there into the next century and beyond. New technology may lessen the need for some manpower, but such technologies are increasingly expensive and will never be able to end the need for the common foot soldier. Forces will be needed not only for the traditionally threatened areas of Europe, Japan and Korea, but also in new areas of potential conflict. Instead of trying to station a large number of troops fully equipped around the world, the US, in order to cut costs and remain flexible, will probably turn more in the direction of conventional units patterned after the Rapid Deployment Force now being prepared for the Middle East and Persian Gulf contingencies.

In the foreseeable future American nuclear strategy will probably remain tied, at least in public mind, to a policy of Mutual Assured Destruction and a secure second strike to deter nuclear war. But it is in the realm of nuclear war that technological advances may have the greatest potential of altering defense policy and strategy. New advances in both Soviet and American weaponry, in ABM technology and lasers for example, could once again make a counterforce strategy viable, make nuclear war theoretically winnable, and, thus, more of a possibility. Any strategic arms reduction talks will be faced with the formidable task of trying not only to reduce existing systems but also to insure that destabilizing future systems are not developed in the first place.

The US Navy's Jeff B landing craft during trials in the Gulf of Mexico in 1979. Experiments in the military use of hovercraft have so far proved relatively disappointing but are symbolic of the military's continuing interest in high technology.

# A NUCLEAR POWER

Above: Dr J. Robert Oppenheimer, wartime director of the Manhattan Project which developed the first nuclear weapons.

Right: Enrico Fermi, under whose direction the first man-made self-sustaining nuclear chain reaction was achieved in laboratories at the University of Chicago in December 1942. Fermi was one of the most important of the Manhattan Project's scientists.

Second right: General Leslie Groves, who was military head of the Manhattan Project, is seen in 1949 shortly before testifying to a Congressional committee investigating leaks of atomic information to the Russians.

Previous page: The familiar mushroom cloud over a 1950s test of a tactical nuclear weapon in Nevada. Such tests eventually led to the production of nuclear weapons with very small yields.

More than any other reason, the United States is a superpower because it is a nuclear power. Natural resource endowments, industrial development and population certainly add to the country's power as does the size of the conventional armed forces. All of these factors put the US in the forefront of world nations. But it is the possession of nuclear weapons and the means to deliver them to any place on earth that raises US military power above that of almost all other countries.

## Nuclear Weapons Development

America's nuclear weapons program actually began before the country entered World War II. Albert Einstein sent his now famous letter to President Roosevelt in October 1939 outlining the possibilities that an atomic bomb could be made. It was not until June of 1942 that the Manhattan Project, the codename for the bomb development program, got underway. To concentrate efforts more and speed up the development process, Washington sent hundreds of top scientists and technicians, who were directly involved in the program, to a laboratory in an isolated part of the New Mexican desert.

Toward the goal of an atomic bomb, these men had to solve the problems of producing enough enriched Uranium or Plutonium fuel and find a way to bring it together in such a way that it would reach critical mass, resulting in an atomic explosion. After discussing and experimenting with a number of refining methods they eventually decided on an enrichment process and centered the major fuel producing efforts at a massive plant at Oak Ridge, Tennessee. The development of a way to reach critical mass turned out to be a much more difficult problem. The first proposed solution became known as the 'gun' system. It involved taking

two pieces of sub-critical nuclear material and firing one into the other thus forming a critical mass. A gun type system was the simplest of designs but was also an inefficient use of nuclear fuel. The second method depended on implosion. A large sphere of nuclear fuel would be surrounded by shaped explosive charges which, when set off simultaneously, would cause the Uranium fuel to implode into itself reaching critical mass. This method promised to be much more efficient than the gun type, but had the drawback that unless the implosion occurred evenly around the entire sphere, critical mass would not be reached. The engineers eventually

decided to pursue both methods in the hope that at least one would work. In the end both worked.

The scientists' efforts were crowned with success in mid-1945. On 14 July the US successfully tested an implosion weapon at the Trinity site in New Mexico. The first actual bomb – Little Boy – was ten and a half feet long and two and a half feet wide, weighed 9700lbs, and used the gun type detonation system. On the morning of 6 August 1945 a B-29 bomber dropped it on Hiroshima, Japan and destroyed 67 percent of the structures, inflicting 135,000 casualties. Three days later another bomber dropped Fat Man, an implosion type weapon weighing 10,000lbs, on and annihilated much of the city of Nagasaki. At that time the US became the first superpower, but its total supply of nuclear weapons consisted of only one bomb left out of the original fuel produced for four.

Most histories of US nuclear weapons development end with the mushroom cloud over the two doomed Japanese cities. In fact the real development of nuclear weaponry for America's superpower status was only beginning in 1945. Immediately after the war, the nuclear weapons program suffered a decline as most of the original scientists at Los Alamos and the rest of the country returned to civilian life. The most serious problem confronting American weapons program after the war, however, was not the loss of scientists, but the lack of nuclear fuel to build, test and perfect better weapons. Plants at Oak Ridge and other parts of the country were built on a crash basis to produce enough fuel quickly for the war project with little thought to mass production of weapons grade fuel after the conflict. Many of the US refining facilities had to be redesigned and rebuilt after the war to provide the material necessary to build a bomb stockpile. Throughout the early postwar years nuclear fuel remained very scarce. Between 1945 and 1950 the US put most of its efforts into building up its nuclear arsenal and very little into testing. America conducted only two tests in 1946 and none in 1947. By the end of 1951 the US had carried out a total of only five nuclear weapon tests since Nagasaki. Even so, the stockpile still grew very slowly. Various estimates indicate that by 1950 the US probably only had between 100 and 150 fission bombs. These were so small that, in total, they probably would have been unable to do more damage than conventional bombing had already done to Germany in World War II.

American scientists directed most of their fission weapon development in the late 1940s and early 1950 toward shrinking the size of the huge bombs developed at Los Alamos. Much of the miniaturization process involved making more efficient use of nuclear fuel – trying to get more bang out of the material involved. Fat Man's implosion device used around 130lbs of Plutonium, in a mass about the size of a football. But scientists thought 15lbs of material were all that was necessary for a critical mass. As little as five pounds would theoretically be enough for a 'trigger quantity'. Scientists also determined that one pound of nuclear fuel – about the size of one square inch – was equal to 4000 tons of conventional TNT explosive power.

The shrinking process continued in the early 1950s and eventually produced results which led to the development of small warheads for tactical nuclear weapons. This coincided with the production of more nuclear fuel for increasing testing. The development of smaller yield nuclear weapons was evident in the series of tests in the early 1950s which featured explo-

Below: A nuclear weapon of the Little Boy type used to attack Hiroshima. Little Boy's explosive yield was roughly equivalent to 12,500 tons of TNT.

Bottom: Scenes of devastation in Hiroshima some 4000 feet from ground zero.

sions in the low kiloton range. One test in 1951 actually had yield of only one tenth of a kiloton (100 tons). In 1953 the US deployed a 280mm atomic cannon to Europe which was capable of firing a tactical nuclear artillery shell.

As soon as many of the problems on shrinking the size of weapons were overcome, scientists turned their attention in just the opposite direction – keeping weapons small but increasing the yield. Once again the problems centered on engineering to make better use of a limited amount of fuel. Efforts in this direction were also successful, for in November 1952 a US bomber dropped a 500 kiloton (one half mega-

Above: An early test of the tactical nuclear shell fired from a US Army 280mm cannon.

Opposite: Test launch of a Douglas SM-75 Thor intermediate-range ballistic missile. The first Thor was delivered to the USAF in 1956 and the system was declared operational in 1959.

ton) bomb – the largest purely fission weapon ever tested. Although the testing of so large a fission weapon was a considerable accomplishment, other advances, which had already pushed US nuclear weapons development into areas far in advance of small fission weapons, totally overshadowed it.

In the late 1940s fission development began to take second place to development of a super-bomb based on the fusion of hydrogen – the hydrogen bomb. Project Panda, as the H-bomb project was known, began in earnest in 1949 largely as a response to the Soviets' first test of an atomic bomb. The first test took place on Eniwetok Atoll in the Pacific on 1 November 1952. The shot disappointed some officials because rather than a practical deliverable bomb, the device was actually the size of a building. Most criticism, however, paled next to the sheer power of the hydrogen device. Scientists had hoped that the "Mike" shot would deliver a few megatons but measurements showed that it actually had the power of around ten and a half million tons of TNT (10.5 megatons). A few months later in March 1954 the US tested a thermonuclear device of over 15 megatons – the largest nuclear device America has ever tested. After three years of further testing, scientists solved the problem of developing a deliverable thermonuclear device when the US tested an air deliverable H-bomb of several megatons in 1956.

The mid-1950s became an era of plenty for American nuclear weapon development prog-

rams. Refining plants reached full output, producing more than enough weapons grade nuclear material to build a large fission and fusion stockpile with enough left over for weapons testing. Testing resulted in the general improvement of nuclear weapons, characterized by a reduction in size while maintaining high yield. A comparison of the early postwar products to those developed in the late 1950s shows how much weapon development really advanced. Fat Man and Little Boy each weighed around five tons. By the mid 1950s the US Air Force had a sleek aerodynamic Mk-7 fission bomb of 2000lbs which could be carried by an F-86 fighter jet. The first thermonuclear bomb, the Mk-17, was a true monster. It weighed over 21 tons, was 24 feet long by 5½ feet in diameter, and had a variable 10 to 25 megaton yield. By the late 1950s the Air Force had the Mk-28 fusion weapon which was only 9 feet long by 20 inches in diameter, weighed 2½ tons, and had a 1 to 20 megaton variable yield.

Nuclear warhead development on missiles also made significant progress. Early warheads were large and bulky in shape with a blunt nose to survive reentry heats. Later warheads, such as those developed for Titan rockets and especially for Minuteman III, were smaller needle-nosed, cone shaped projectiles that presented a small radar cross section and plunged through the atmosphere at high speed with better accuracy. Although the early Atlas warheads weighed tons, a single 170 kiloton yield reentry vehicle on the MIRV bus of a Minuteman III missile weighs only a few hundred pounds. The new warheads for the MX missile will be the same size as those of Minuteman III yet will more than double the explosive power to 350 kilotons.

One of the most significant advances of the nuclear weapons research in the 1960s and 1970s was the development of the enhanced radiation weapon or neutron bomb. This device is basically a small fission/fusion weapon which expends most of its power in initial radiation and not in blast and thermal effects. A one kiloton neutron weapon delivers the same radiation effect that a 15 kiloton fission weapon gives but without all the blast effects. The remarkable thing about neutron weapons is that scientists could actually produce a fusion weapon in a low kiloton and even sub-kiloton range for use in the tactical battlefield.

## The Triad
The basis of postwar US nuclear strategy is deterrence through Mutually Assured Destruction. A fundamental aspect of this strategy is that the US must maintain a secure nuclear force that can wreak unacceptable retaliatory damage on the Soviets. The need for a secure second strike capability to back up the deterrence strategy became evident in the mid 1950s and, along with evolving technology in weaponry and delivery systems, gradually led to a mutually supporting group of three nuclear weapons systems – the Triad.

Each of the members of the Triad – land based ICBMs, submarine launched ballistic missiles (SLBMs), and manned bombers – had advantages and disadvantages that the others lacked. Long range, later intercontinental manned bombers had the advantages of large payload, could be recalled after take off, and could change course and targets in flight. Unfortunately they could be destroyed at their bases in a surprise first strike, were dependent on tanker aircraft, and had to fight their way through increasingly deadly Soviet air defenses. ICBMs could be launched quickly and escape destruction on the ground and no enemy defense was capable of stopping a missile warhead from streaking down and hitting its targets. Missiles, however, were initially unreliable, once launched could not be recalled, and over time became increasingly threatened by a Soviet counterforce capability. Missiles aboard submarines promised to be the most survivable member of the Triad since it was virtually impossible for the enemy to locate a submarine. It was difficult, however, for the command center in Washington to communicate with its submarine force and the early missiles had a short range and were inaccurate.

Together, all three systems contributed to a nuclear force entailing a secure second strike which the Soviets could not destroy. A sneak attack on the bombers would still leave the SLBMs and ICBMs intact. Attempts to hunt

Above: The submarine USS *Grayback* enters San Diego harbor with a Regulus I missile positioned on the launch ramp. The 400-mile range Regulus I cruise missile was kept in service until 1964.

Right: The B-47 bomber was the backbone of SAC in the 1950s and some remained in service until the early years of the Vietnam War.

Far right, bottom: An early B-52 in flight. In progressively improved versions the B-52 has already seen almost 30 years of service. The most recent B-52G and H versions will probably soldier on into the 1990s.

down the SLBMs at sea would alert the bombers and ICBMs. In short, the Triad was a good answer to needs of a nuclear power searching for a secure second strike.

## Bombers

The US bomber force is the oldest member of the Triad and the only one ever actually to carry out a nuclear strike. The combination of the B-29 bomber and the atomic bomb attacks on Hiroshima and Nagasaki launched airpower into a place of preeminence in the American defense establishment. It is no surprise that the Strategic Air Command (SAC), which has responsibility for strategic bombers (and later land based ICBMs) was formed in 1946 – a year before its parent organization, the US Air Force, was set up as the third branch of the US armed forces.

America's first strategic bombers were those left over from World War II pressed into service in a new role with only mixed success. The B-29 Superfortress was the first US nuclear bomber but this occurred more out of a need to find a plane large enough to carry the first atomic bombs than anything else. SAC received its first post-war bomber in 1948 when the B-36 Peacemaker became operational. This giant aircraft, designed for use in World War II, was huge and dwarfed even the later B-52 Stratofortress and B-1 jet bombers.

Less than 350 B-29s and B-36s actually entered service with SAC. The main reason for this small deployment was that both aircraft lacked long range and were not really intercontinental without extensive foreign basing or in-flight refueling. More importantly, both planes were slow prop-driven dinosaurs at the dawn of the jet age. By the early 1950s both the US and the Soviet Union had tested and deployed new jet fighter aircraft which promised to make short work of the huge slow bombers. Such advances made it questionable whether the B-36 or B-29 would ever be able to penetrate Soviet defenses and deliver their bombs on target.

The short-term answer to the SAC's critical needs came in the form of the B-47 Stratojet bomber. This aircraft was considerably ahead of

Below: A Boeing B-50 Superfortress, a much improved version of the World War II B-29, which was a mainstay of SAC during the command's early years.

its time technologically, incorporating swept back wings, with six jet engines, and a very small three-man crew. More importantly, however, the B-47 was designed specifically to carry nuclear weapons. Its main drawback was a short 2000 mile range and the planes needed bases in Europe to reach targets in the USSR. Still, the B-47 proved to be the most successful bomber not only in SAC but also in the American postwar Air Force. The US built over 2000 planes up to 1957 when production ceased. The large numbers of B-47s that rolled off the production lines in the mid 1950s ended the so-called bomber gap because by 1955 SAC had over 1500 bombers, 1300 of which were B-47s.

Perhaps the landmark year for SAC came in 1955. Not only were large numbers of B-47s entering service but the US also received its first truly intercontinental bomber – the B-52 Stratofortress. Since then this bomber has become the oldest part of the Triad. The eight engined B-52 was unique because it could strike anywhere in the Soviet Union carrying four Mk-28 thermonuclear weapons each with a 20

megaton yield. Thus every B-52 carried more destructive explosive equivalent in its bomb bay than had been expended by all the aircraft of the world in the previous history of air warfare. Its six-man crew could push the plane to a top speed of over 600mph and a ceiling of 55,000 feet. Between 1955 and 1962 the US built a total of 744 B-52s in various models adding new advances as they became available. With the addition of the Stratofortress the bomber leg of the Triad reached its peak in 1959 when SAC counted over 1850 B-47s and B-52s in its inventory at 65 bases; 40 in the US and 25 overseas.

Following the heyday of the 1950s, however, the bomber began to slip into decline in the Triad. This resulted primarily because of the advent of the land-based ICBMs and SLBMs in the American strategic nuclear inventory. More importantly, in the early 1960s American strategists began to question the survivability of bombers in the face of the growing threat from land based Soviet ICBMs which could theoretically destroy SAC's bombers at their bases before the planes ever took off. This fear

Below: A B-52H refuels from a KC-135 Stratotanker. Aerial refueling plays a vital part in giving tactical flexibility to the strategic bomber force. The USAF has over 600 KC-135s in service with support of the strategic bomber force as their first priority mission.

Left: The crew of a B-52G
board their aircraft during
an alert. The two blisters
under the aircraft's chin are
where the low light TV and
forward looking infra-red
systems are mounted. These
play a vital part in helping
the B-52 operate at low level
in all weather conditions.

The Ballistic Missile Early Warning System station at Thule in Greenland. The old BMEWS and Distant Early Warning (DEW) systems remain a vital part of US strategic defenses.

was compounded in 1960 when an American U-2 reconnaissance aircraft, flying much higher than a B-52, was shot down by a Soviet surface-to-air-missile (SAM). Not only were bombers therefore seen as vulnerable at their bases, but there was also a question as to whether bombers could get to their target.

In answer to the penetrability/base vulnerability question, SAC came up with a number of plans or new plane designs, none of which really solved the problems. In order to lessen base vulnerability, SAC put aircraft on alert status to take off within fifteen minutes of warning. In times of tension, such as during the Cuban missiles crisis, they were to be dispersed to civilian airfields to make them less vulnerable to attack or a portion of the force would be kept constantly in the air ready to fly toward their targets. To penetrate Soviet defense, the American engineers designed and produced a limited number of two new jet bombers. The medium range B-58 Hustler was supposed to penetrate Soviet air space and defenses at over 1400 miles per hour. A new intercontinental bomber – the B-70

– was designed and test flown as a plane that could fly in Soviet airspace at very high altitudes and speeds. Secretary of Defense McNamara, however, had little faith in the viability of the manned penetrating bomber, and the US deployed only about 100 B-58s and cancelled the B-70 program before production.

Throughout the 1960s and 1970s the B-52 continued to be the only intercontinental bomber in the Triad. In order to keep these increasingly aged aircraft serviceable and to increase their capabilities, the planes underwent various structural and electronic improvements over the years. Still, time began to take its toll and by 1982 the number of operating Stratofortresses had shrunk to 300.

The advance of technology in the late 1960s and early 1970s began to give indications that the bomber still might be a valuable member of the Triad. The development of variable geometry swing wings, first pioneered on the medium range FB-111, made possible jet aircraft that could not only fly effectively at high altitude and supersonic speeds but also hug the ground

cancelled the B-1A, the Reagan Administration has given new life to this part of SAC by initiating plans to restart the B-1B program. Although the new bomber is smaller than the B-52 it can carry more payload whether in conventional bombs, cruise missiles, SRAMs or a combination of all three. It has longer range than the B-52, can fly higher, and has a top speed of over Mach 1.2. Variable geometry swing wings enable the plane to fly high at fast speeds or drop down and hug the ground to avoid enemy radar.

## ICBMs

America's first nuclear weapon-carrying ballistic missiles actually were not ICBMs but shorter range intermediate and medium range ballistic missiles. The early Thor and Jupiter rockets developed by the Army and Air Force in the early 1950s owed much to the German V-2s. The Army's Jupiter developed in 1955 carried a one megaton warhead 2000 miles. The US eventually deployed 60 of these missiles in Turkey and Italy between 1960 and 1965. Using off-the-shelf technology, the Air Force developed the Thor in only one year. Thors had roughly the same characteristics as the Jupiter and between 1959 and 1963 the US based a limited number of them in England. Both Jupiter and Thor suffered considerable handicaps, however, because

Short Range Attack Missiles being prepared for service. The SRAM has been credited with a range in excess of 100 miles and speed greater than Mach 3 although performance varies greatly depending on the flight path which the missile has been programmed to follow.

and escape radar and penetrate to their targets. Bomber capabilities increased even more with the deployment of Short Range Attack Missiles (SRAMs) and later long range cruise missiles. SRAMs, with their 200 kiloton warheads, allowed bombers to destroy enemy fighter bases, radar sites, or SAM sites miles ahead of the attacking bomber, thus clearing a path for the planes. Small air launched cruise missiles have a range of 750 to 1500 miles. Because of their unique radar guidance system they can skim 100 feet above the ground, making them difficult if not impossible to shoot down. The same guidance system gives the missile the capability of putting its 100 kiloton warhead to within 300 feet of a target. Cruise missiles completely end the need for a bomber to penetrate enemy airspace and allow the plane to launch its missiles outside SAM and fighter range.

The US put all of these technological advances into the new B-1 bomber developed in the mid 1970s. Although the Carter Administration dealt what appeared to be a mortal blow to the manned bomber leg of the Triad when it

Left: An FB-111A in flight with an SRAM in the internal weapons bay. Additional SRAMs can be carried on wing pylons.

Below: An FB-111A takes off. The strategic bomber FB-111 is slightly larger and heavier than the versions deployed in the tactical role. SAC operates five squadrons of FB-111s with a total of some 60 aircraft.

of short range and system vulnerability. They were never considered for wide deployment but were only a stop-gap measure until real ICBMs could be developed.

Atlas, America's first true ICBMs, made the second land-based missile leg of the Triad a reality. In 1954 the Air Force restarted development of the missile, which had been halted in the early 1950s, and the first test model flew successfully in June 1957, five months before Sputnik. The giant liquid fuel rocket, 88 feet long and 10 feet wide, was made up of over 100,000 parts and could carry a 3 megaton warhead 6000 miles. Its early radio and later radio/

Right: A Minuteman III missile in its silo at Vandenberg AFB, California. Minuteman III weighs some 76,000 pounds at launch and has a maximum range of 8000 miles.

Second right: A Minuteman is loaded into a silo at Edwards AFB during testing of the missile.

inertial guidance system gave it a rough accuracy of 3 miles – good enough to hit most Soviet cities.

The first Atlases became operational in 1958 but many officials immediately claimed that the system was highly vulnerable to Soviet attack. The first Atlas bases were above ground. The supporting facilities, to say nothing of the delicate missile itself, were very vulnerable to the shock and overpressure of a nuclear explosion even many miles away. To reduce the vulnerability, SAC first put the missiles below ground horizontally in coffin-like shelters and later put them in huge underground silos. (In both cases launchers raised the missiles to the surface just before launch.) Engineers used reinforced concrete to harden the silos to withstand 100psi. overpressure or the equivalent of a one megaton nuclear explosion as close as 3500 feet away.

Even with these protective measures, however, the early Atlas ICBMs were crude weapons and suffered from considerable drawbacks. Since the missile used highly volatile liquid propellant, they had to be completely

fueled just before launch which took between 20 and 30 minutes; long enough for a Soviet warhead to arrive. Because of its vulnerabilities, the US deployed only 176 Atlases in various models up to 1964. By 1965 most of them were already being phased out in favor of new, more advanced ICBMs.

The US developed Titan ICBMs roughly in the same period of the 1950s, but because this missile appeared in an advanced second mode strategists consider it to be a second generation US ICBM. Like Atlas, Titan I also used volatile liquid fuel. At 100 feet by 10 feet it was much more powerful and carried a single 18 megaton warhead – the largest ever deployed on a US missile. It also had a more accurate guidance system with an accuracy of around one mile. Engineers largely eliminated Titan I's liquid fuel vulnerability by the development of a storable liquid fuel system in the Titan II which allowed the propellant to remain in the missile for long periods. This change reduced the firing time from around half an hour to a few minutes. Both Titans were designed to be fired from underground silos. Although Titan I had to be raised to the surface, Titan II could be ignited and launched from inside the silo, thus increasing its survivability. A total of 63 Titan Is was deployed by 1963 but by 1965 the Air Force began to phase them out in favor of 54 Titan IIs. Fifty-three Titan IIs, with newer guidance systems and warheads, are still in service with SAC. Problems with Titan II, even with a storable liquid fuel missile, were evident in the catastrophic explosion of one missile in 1980.

Titan and Atlas deployment were deliberately kept low in the 1960s because by the late 1950s US defense officials made the fundamental decision to base American ICBM forces on solid fuel Minuteman missiles. Minuteman was the result of the same solid fuel technology in the 1950s that also led to the successful development of the Polaris submarine launched missiles. Minuteman I, three stages, 60 feet long and 5 feet wide, was much smaller than Atlas and Titan. Even so it still could carry a one megaton warhead intercontinental distances. After a series of successful test flights in 1959 it became operational in 1962.

The massive deployment of Minuteman between 1962 and 1965 – over 800 missiles at five SAC bases – attests to its great success and also to the extent of the nuclear build up ordered by the Kennedy Administration. All of the missiles went into underground silos hardened to withstand 300psi, protecting them against a one megaton blast as close as a half-mile away. Two Air Force officers in an underground command center control a flight of ten missiles. The Defense Department discussed other basing modes, such as putting the missiles on railroad cars, but these ideas were later dismissed as impractical. Minuteman proved to be so suc-

cessful that the Air Force originally planned to deploy over 3000 but by the mid 1960s Secretary MacNamara concluded that the US had enough ICBMs. American land based missile strength peaked in 1967 at 1054 Minuteman and Titan missiles; 1000 Minutemen and 53 Titans remain deployed today.

Minuteman missiles have undergone two significant improvements since deployment. The first occurred in 1964 when the Minuteman II appeared consisting of a new second stage, larger two megaton warhead, and improved guidance and decoy system designed to foil any Soviet anti-ballistic missile system. Beginning in 1966 SAC deployed the first of 450 Minuteman IIs. Perhaps the most important improvement, however, was the development of Multiple Independently-targetable Reentry Vehicle systems (or MIRV) in what eventually became known as the Minuteman III. This MIRV warhead system allows one missile to carry more than one warhead and deliver it with greater accuracy. The MIRV system on the present Minuteman III carries three warheads and although each has only 170 kiloton yield, the ability to strike within a quarter mile of the target makes up for the loss of explosive power. The US has deployed 550 Minuteman IIIs.

MIRVing Minuteman and putting MIRVs on missiles of the future raised a considerable con-

A 40 second timed exposure taken from a US Navy aircraft showing the impact of the various sections of a Trident C4 reentry vehicle during a 1980 test. MIRV warheads can attack a wider spread of targets than is suggested by this picture.

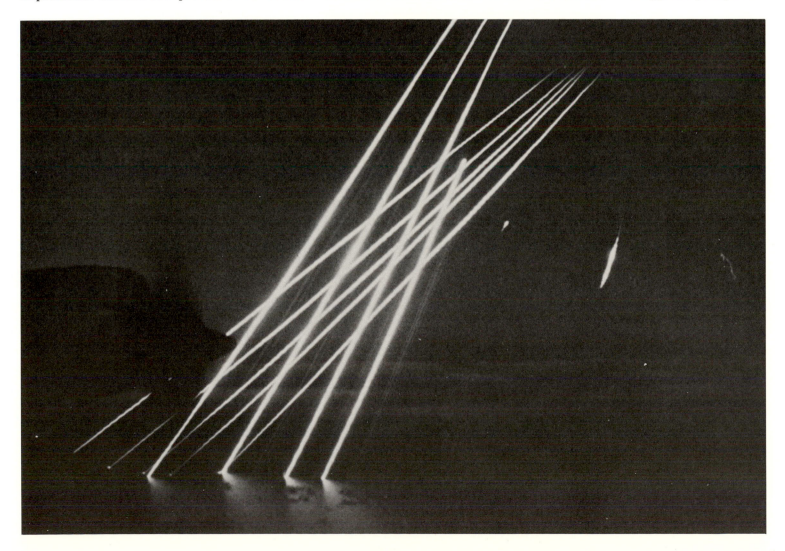

Opposite: An MX, Peacekeeper missile, undergoes vibration tests late in 1982.

Right: The nose cone and MIRV warheads of the MX during testing of the system for separating the nose cone to allow the warheads to deploy to their individual targets.

Below: Artist's impression of the controversial Dense Pack basing mode for the MX system.

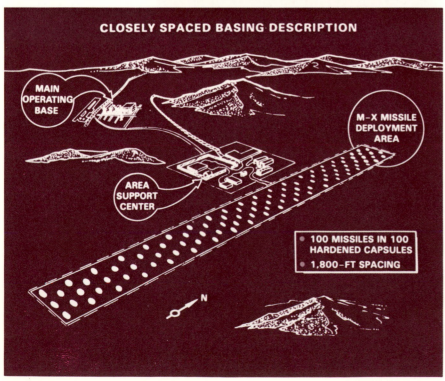

**CLOSELY SPACED BASING DESCRIPTION**

MAIN OPERATING BASE

M-X MISSILE DEPLOYMENT AREA

AREA SUPPORT CENTER

- 100 MISSILES IN 100 HARDENED CAPSULES
- 1,800-FT SPACING

N

troversy in the US. Many felt the system signaled a US move toward a counterforce capability. The original rationale for MIRV was that they were necessary to overwhelm any Soviet ABM system. With 1000s of warheads to contend with in a very short time, any Soviet anti-missile interceptor system would soon be exhausted. But the increased accuracy of MIRV also made it possible for SAC to destroy Soviet silos. When the US signed the SALT I Treaty, many critics stated that there was no need for MIRVs. By that time the system was already too far along in development to be stopped. Those in favor of MIRV contended that there was considerable need for the US to have at least some of the counterforce capability offered by MIRV.

Even though Minuteman underwent extensive improvement in the 1960s, it was clear by the mid 1970s that the US needed a completely new ICBM. Minuteman's proposed successor the new MX missile, for Missile eXperimental, was designed to be more survivable in addition to having increased range and payload. Although it weighs three times as much as Minuteman III, MX is only slightly longer and will be able to fit into old Minuteman silos. Every missile will carry a MIRV system with ten warheads, each with a yield of 350 kilotons, to within 600 feet of its targets. An MX missile is accurate enough to travel 6000 miles and hit a target the size of an average city block with a warhead 20 times more powerful than the bomb which destroyed much of Hiroshima. This combination also means that, theoretically, it would take only 300 MX missiles to destroy every land based Soviet ICBM.

A continuing controversy around the MX is how it will be based. Soviet missiles also have improved accuracy and much if not all of the US silo-based missile system will become vulnerable to enemy attack. The two most famous MX basing plans entailed placing each of the missiles in a circular underground race-way or to have each one moved from one to another of 20 identical shelters in a kind of shell game in which the Soviets would never know the real location of the missiles. Another alternative was to keep the missile aboard airplanes and launch them while airborne. The Reagan Administration rejected the race way and shell games alternatives because of the land they would take up (the shell game would need an area the size of Connecticut) and because of civilian opposition to the proposed bases in Nevada and New Mexico. Another suggested MX basing method is to place the missiles in superhardened silos relatively close together. In this so called Dense Pack mode the Soviets could not destroy many of the missiles in a massive first strike because the first Soviet warhead, exploding near the target, would destroy or knock off course the other incoming Soviet warheads allowing a large number of MXs to survive.

## SLBMs

Submarine Launched Ballistic Missiles (SLBMs) are the third leg of the Triad and represent one of the most successful and invulnerable strategic weapons in the US nuclear arsenal. Developed in the 1950s the SLBM system took advantage of the simultaneous development of nuclear powered submarines, solid fuel rocket engines, and small nuclear warheads to produce a unique marriage of submersible ship and long range nuclear tipped missile – the ideal secure second strike retaliatory weapon.

Work on the first US Polaris SSBN (Submersible Ship Ballistic Nuclear), began in 1955.

The ship was actually a nuclear powered attack submarine which had been cut in half with two rows of eight missile tubes added. Each tube held a 30 foot Polaris missile and launched it while the ship was submerged. The new submarine stretched out to 381 feet and displaced 6800 tons when submerged. They were designed to spend all of the time underwater and at 25 knots actually were faster beneath the waves than on the surface. Each Polaris A-1 missile had a range of 1300 miles carrying a half megaton warhead with an accuracy of around a mile. The original plan called for the first SSBN with its missiles to be operational and on station sometime in 1963 but the program progressed so well that the first Polaris sub – the *George Washington* – went on station in November 1960.

The Navy quickly went ahead with production of SSBNs, eventually launching 41 boats although the admirals wanted 45. The total number of missiles reached a peak of 656 when the US launched the last boat, the *Will Rodgers,* in 1967. In order to get the maximum protection from the force, the US keeps half of the fleet at sea at any one time. A boat stays out for tours of 60 to 100 days, being on station – within range of its targets in the USSR – for most of this period. Maintenance and testing schedules are designed so that each boat at sea has at least 14

Below: A ballistic missile submarine on the surface with the hatches on eight of the sixteen missile tubes open. The missiles would normally be fired when the submarine is submerged.

Right: The USS *Nathan Hale* (SSBN.623), one of the *Lafayette* class, was built to carry 16 Polaris missiles but was modified later to accept the Poseidon system.

Below: Spectacular surface launch of a Polaris A-2 missile from the USS *Henry Clay* (SSBN.625) in 1964. The submarine's list to port is part of the surface launch procedure. The tall mast fitted on the sail carries electronic equipment specially installed to monitor the test. The debris flying around the missile comes from launch adapters which held the missile in position in its tube.

of the 16 missiles always ready for firing. Polaris submarines hold the distinction of being the only missile member of the Triad ever to launch a missile carrying a nuclear weapon, during a test in 1962.

Like the other members of the Triad, SLBMs and SSBNs have undergone considerable system improvements over the years since the Navy deployed the first boat. Four classes of SSBNs, *George Washington, Ethan Allan, Lafayette* and *Benjamin Franklin*, were eventually built for the Polaris and later Poseidon missiles. New navigation aids, allowing the submarine to determine its position more accurately and thus deliver its missile warheads more accurately, were introduced. The Navy has also tried to deploy ultra-low frequency radio communications systems to communicate with deeply submerged submarines.

The most important improvements, however, have come in the new missiles deployed on SSBNs. Work on the Polaris A-2 missile began in 1959 with a first flight in 1960. The new missiles fitted the same launch tube but increased the range to 1700 miles allowing the subs to hit the same targets but cruise on station further from the Soviet coasts. Polaris A-3 missiles appeared in the mid 1960s and took advantage of more efficient fuels to boost the range to 2800 miles. Moreover, this missile also incorporated three Multiple Reentry Vehicles (MRVs) with a yield of 300 kilotons each. Although unguided and relatively inaccurate, the MRV warheads could strike three widely scattered targets. Advanced technology in the late 1960s made the Poseidon missile possible with a first test flight in 1968 and operational deployment on US submarines in 1971. The new missile was significantly larger than the Polaris missile so the submarine had to undergo launch tube modification. Thirty-one newer Polaris subs underwent these changes and became Poseidon SSBNs. Like Polaris A-3 each Poseidon missile had a range of 2800 miles but featured a MIRV system incorporating 10 to 14 warheads, each of 50 kilotons yield, with an accuracy of about one half mile. The Poseidon program and its MIRVed system thus gave the US a total of over 5000 warheads on its submarine leg of the Triad alone.

The greatest improvement to the SSBN fleet came in the early 1970s when the government made the decision to build an entirely new advanced nuclear missile firing submarine. Defense officials judged that by the 1980s the original Polaris boats would reach the end of the estimated 20 year hull life and new ships would be needed. Advances in Soviet anti-submarine warfare technology, especially in hunter killer submarines, led to the order that attention should be given to the development of SSBNs that were not only much quieter but also carried longer range missiles to give the boats more ocean to hide in. The discussion came down to a decision on whether to build a large number of

Left: A Polaris A-3 missile is launched from the USS *Patrick Henry*. Submarine launched missiles are ejected from their launch tubes by gas pressure with the rocket motor igniting as the missile breaks surface.

Opposite: Four views of the USS *Ohio*, first of the Trident missile submarines. The main picture shows the interior of the missile compartment on the *Ohio*. Inset left, the canister used to load the missiles; inset center, a missile technician at a control room console; top, the *Ohio* on the surface.

A Tomahawk cruise missile
is launched at the Utah Test
and Training Range.
Versions of the General
Dynamics Tomahawk have
been selected by the US
Navy and for the ground-
launched mission shown
here. However, the Air
Force preferred the Boeing
AGM-86 for its strategic
bombers. The AGM-86B
entered service in 1982 but
early in 1983 it was
announced that in the mid
1980s it would be
superceded by weapons
employing the so-called
Stealth technology.

smaller class nuclear SSBNs or to build a few very large boats. Despite considerable criticism from opponents that the larger boats were more vulnerable and costly than the smaller class, the Nixon Administration made the decision to build the large boats resulting in the *Ohio* class Trident submarines.

Each of the ten Trident class ships authorized so far will truly be of Olympian size. At 16,000 tons submerged and 560 feet long these ships are larger than the cruisers used by the US in World War II. They will carry 24 of the new Trident I SLBMs. These missiles have a range of 4300 miles and carry eight to ten 100 kiloton MRIVed warheads with an accuracy of around a quarter mile. There are also plans to produce a Trident-II missile which will have a range of over 6000 miles and an accuracy of less than a quarter mile. The new accuracy will add a whole new dimension to the submarine aspect of the Triad allowing SLBMs to destroy hardened targets.

Cruise missiles could be placed not only on SSBNs but also on the 90 other US nuclear attack submarines thus making every US boat capable of strategic nuclear strikes. Such a growth of forces would significantly worsen the Soviets' anti-submarine warfare problems.

## Future of the Triad
The role of the US land based missile leg of the Triad has always, at least in public mind, been one of retaliation. As the accuracy of missiles has improved, however, their targets probably have changed from cities to more important military targets like command centers, missile silos or army bases. This would be the role of ICBMs today even in a second strike attack. It has become important for the US to destroy such targets in order to blunt or destroy Moscow's warfighting capabilities even after a Soviet first strike. In a sense, to deter in the future the US must be prepared to make a counterforce strike on the enemy forces, showing him he cannot win a military victory even at the price of having his cities destroyed.

The key future problem confronting American ICBMs is that all silo based missiles will

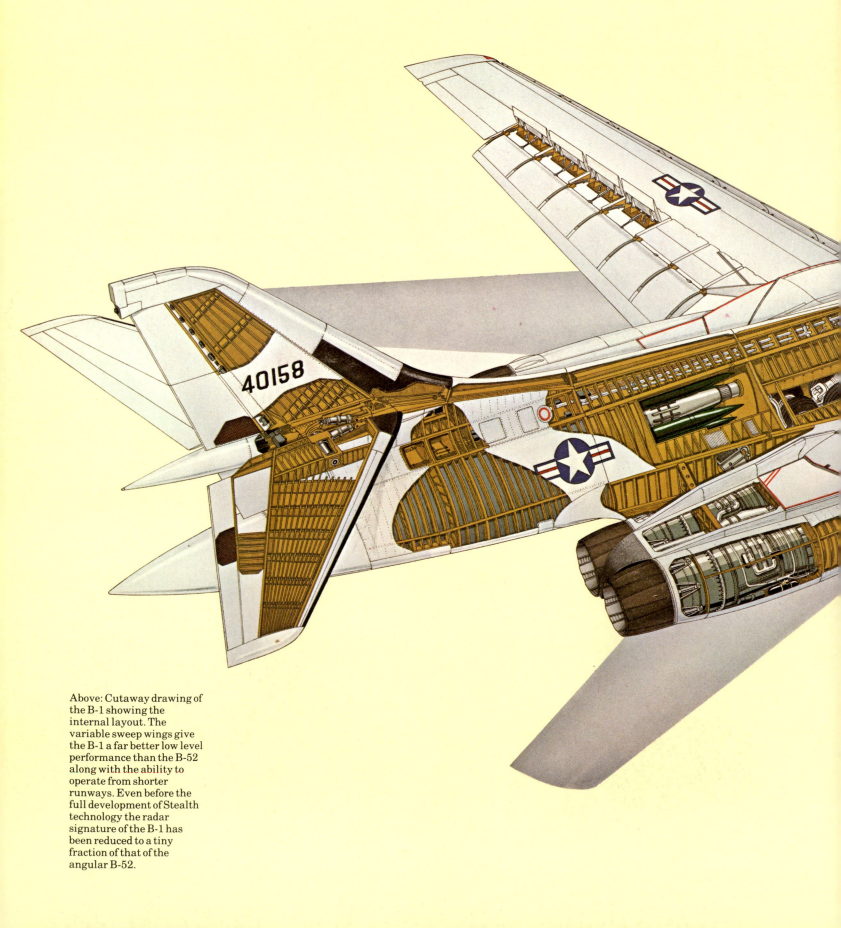

Above: Cutaway drawing of
the B-1 showing the
internal layout. The
variable sweep wings give
the B-1 a far better low level
performance than the B-52
along with the ability to
operate from shorter
runways. Even before the
full development of Stealth
technology the radar
signature of the B-1 has
been reduced to a tiny
fraction of that of the
angular B-52.

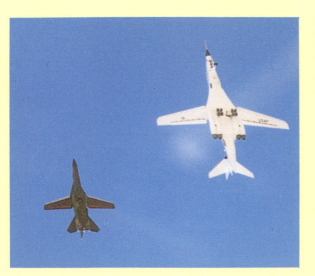

Left: The B-1 bomber seen during its first test flight in company with a much smaller F-111.

Above: One of the B-1A prototypes in flight. The B-1B differs from the earlier model in being considerably heavier with longer range but reduced maximum speed.

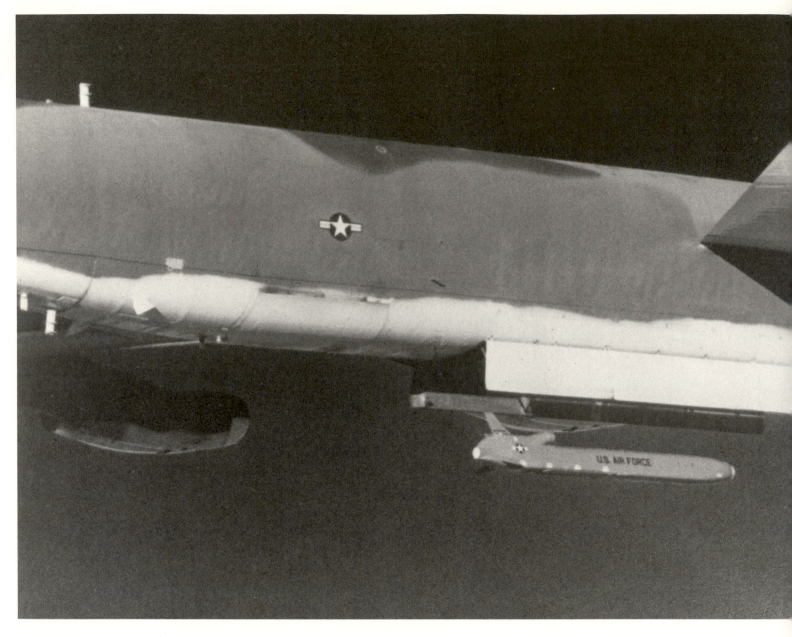

A cruise missile is launched from the internal bomb bay of a B-52. The AGM-86B which is entering service is credited with a range of up to 1500 miles and is believed to carry a 200 kiloton warhead in the strategic version.

become vulnerable to attack. It will be difficult for the future American ICBM force to survive and carry out any role in the Triad. This problem lies, however, not in the vulnerability of its bases but in how the US intends to respond to an attack. In the past the accepted strategy has always been to try to build a system that can ride out or survive a Soviet first strike. With increased Soviet silo busting capabilities this may no longer be feasible or safe. Instead of trying to ride out the Soviet first strike, the President, at the first confirmation of a Soviet mass launch, could immediately launch all US missiles before the enemy warheads arrived. Soviet weapons would then attack empty silos. This launch-on-warning capability has been proposed in the past but officials rejected it as too risky because the US might accidentally launch all its missiles after a false alarm. With the advance of satellite surveillance technology, however, the President could now be more sure of a real enemy launch. By such an alteration in the proposed response to a Soviet attack, the US could greatly lessen the vulnerability of

its own missiles and give considerable pause to Soviet planners trying to destroy American missile forces.

Despite continuing questions on the viability of the manned bomber, this leg of America's nuclear deterrent system is still effective and worth the continuing expense. If even a small number of bombers, such as the B-1, were to escape destruction at their bases, they might actually be the winning factor in a nuclear war. Because of the adaptability of bombers to changing situations and targets, they would be our most flexible weapon either to threaten the Soviets with further city destruction or carry out attacks on military targets that were still a threat to the US. New weapons in the future might add even more to the bombers' effectiveness. Huge converted 747 airliners could carry and launch over 100 cruise missiles against the USSR. The development and deployment of a new bomber employing 'Stealth' technology – making the plane almost invisible to radar – could add even more viability to the role of the manned penetrating bomber.

Early American Polaris submarines missiles were inaccurate and their role in war – as a secure second strike force to destroy Soviet cities – was clear. As new technology produced more accurate SLBMs and cruise missiles the countervalue role of American SLBMs has begun to blur. MIRVs on SLBMs have now become so accurate that even they can destroy a Soviet missile silo. Moreover, if submarines launch missiles fairly close to the Soviet coast on a depressed trajectory, there would only be minimum warning of attack. Such factors also hold true for the new Soviet long range SSBNs which can attack US silos and bomber bases in a similar way. From beginning as a secure second strike weapon used only after the land based missiles have been launched and the bombers have taken off, the future SLBM may be considered sneak attack weapons to spearhead a counterforce offensive.

It is evident that the US has taken many steps to keep each leg of the Triad viable over the past twenty years. New bombers ICBMs, and submarines have been developed and the old systems have been improved. Despite all the research and development and money spent, each leg of the Triad is more vulnerable to a counterforce strike by the Soviets today than the original members of the Triad were in the early 1960s. The new American weapons are also much more capable of carrying out effective counterforce strikes on the Soviet Union. The security of the individual members of the Triad will probably continue to shrink in the future as new systems, especially those designed for warfare in outer space, are developed. Together, however, the three members will still provide an acceptable measure of security for the US and a large measure of worry for, and therefore a deterrent to, the Soviets.

The E-4A airborne command posts are based on the Boeing 747 airliner but are packed with highly sophisticated communications equipment and will be used by the President and leaders of the military in the event of a Soviet attack.

# THE ARMY

The modern United States Army has been formed by a combination of internal political forces and constraints, changing weaponry, missions, strategy, and assessments of potential enemy capabilities. Ironically, since World War II the Army has always seemed to become involved in wars or interventions in areas where it was not designed to fight. The question that has constantly plagued policy makers over the last forty years is whether the US Army will be able to fight adequately in future wars, especially since it has become more and more apparent that unlike past wars, there will be little time to restructure or rearm the forces once combat begins.

### The Postwar US Army

Until recently America's army has traditionally been very small in peacetime. It was only modernized, armed, and expanded to become a mass army in time of war. The pressure to follow the traditional expansion and contraction cycle was especially intense following World War II. New responsibilities around the world, howev-

Above: Thanksgiving Dinner on the banks of the Yalu River, Korea 1950.

Right: A tired soldier of the 5th Infantry pauses for rest after a long spell in the front line.

Previous page: Infantrymen advance with support from an M60 tank during an exercise.

er, required a large standing army in order for the US to fulfill its new role as leader of the free world. But the pressures from civilians to return to 'normalcy' after the war and the mistaken assumption that the US could rely on nuclear weapons to provide firepower instead of men in uniform caused Washington to cut the Army yet again. In 1946 the Army was reduced from 7 million to 1.8 million men. In 1947 it had fallen to 900,000. By 1948 it was down to an all time postwar low of 550,000 men.

This still left the United States with the largest postwar army it had ever had. But the force was far too small to accomplish the needed tasks of defending Europe, occupying Japan and guarding American interests in the Middle East according to the requirements of the Truman Doctrine set forward by the President in 1948. Some military and civilian leaders recognized that by the late 1940s the Army had grown too

small. In 1948 the Selective Service Act was signed which by 1950 had raised Army manpower to 600,000. The Army, however, was still too small and spread too thinly in all areas to provide a convincing defense or deterrent. Many experts claim that in retrospect the inadequate Army and our over extended defense commitments invited aggression.

The belated recognition of the need for more ground forces almost came too late when American military power was put to the test in the Korean war. Korea came very close to being a blitzkrieg defeat for the US. Ironically, it showed that while the US military is often accused of preparing to fight future wars by preparing for those of the past, it was actually too much reliance on a weapon of the future – the atomic bomb – that almost destroyed US forces and led to a communist victory.

At the start of the war in June 1950, the US Army was abysmally prepared for conventional conflict. The Army had ten divisions of dubious quality patterned after the '1943 model' division based on three regiments. Unfortunately, most of these regiments had only two battalions which were often manned with only a portion of the men they were supposed to have to be combat ready. Many of the veterans who had fought in World War II had left the service and taken their valuable combat experience with them.

The men who entered Korea initially were poorly trained and ineffectively led. The divisions were predominantly equipped with light infantry weapons with little or no mobility. More importantly, the weaponry that was supplied largely was World War II surplus and not up to the advances made in the postwar years. While the Soviets supplied the North Koreans with relatively modern weapons, such as jet aircraft, US troops used weapons – particularly antitank weapons – which were old and ineffective.

Perhaps equally important to the unpreparedness of the US Army was the disinclination of the country as a whole to become involved in a new war. There was little motivation among Americans to fight in Korea. Although the threat to Japan if South Korea should fall was clearly understood by the men in the Truman Administration, the sentiment in the country at large was predominantly against becoming involved in another war so soon after World War II. The average American citizen could not see how a war 10,000 miles away in a small Asian country threatened the peace and security of the US – a fundamental weakness that was to appear in a different war in the late 1960s.

It was no surprise then that the initial combat operations of the US Army in Korea bordered very close to disaster. The initial retreat of US forces and the loss of men and materiel were comparable to the early humiliating defeats of Union forces at the beginning of the Civil War. Luckily, concentrating the remaining Amer-

ican and South Korean forces in the lower end of the peninsula allowed the Allies to stiffen their defenses and halt the northern advance while a toehold remained.

Part of the Army's early problems in the Korean war can be linked to the inability of the Administration to make an early decision on what type of war it sought to wage. Once Washington ruled out the use of nuclear weapons it had no alternative but to depend on the ground forces of the US Army to bear the brunt of the task of regaining lost territory. In the beginning, however, the key role of the ground forces was not recognized and the

Above: Generals MacArthur and Ridgway seen on a visit to the front in 1951. At this time MacArthur was Commander in Chief of the United Nations forces while Ridgway led the Eighth Army.

Left: Men of the 179th Infantry, 45th Division man a snowy front line trench near Chorwon, Korea, 2 January 1952.

Right: A machine gun team of the 5th Marines, 1st Marine Division exchanges fire with North Vietnamese forces in 1968.

strategy was largely to depend on naval and especially conventional air power somehow to halt the enemy. The influence of air power, in the form of strategic bombing, was particularly strong and probably delayed the build up of the Army.

Recognition gradually dawned on the American government that Korea must be a war fought and won on the ground with conventional forces. Once this important idea was accepted by the leadership, the necessary changes in the US Army were made. Of perhaps greatest importance was the reinstitution of the draft. Although unpopular, especially in the Korean situation, conscription supplied the masses of manpower necessary to fill out the depleted ranks of the Army. Eventually 20 full strength divisions were manned. Nine of these were sent to Korea and the remaining eleven were held in reserve in the United States and in Europe in preparation for any potential attacks by the Soviets in other parts of the world – particularly across into West Germany.

Key changes were also made in the leadership of the American Army in Korea. General Matthew Ridgway took command of American forces in the theater and immediately began making personnel and command changes in order to initiate new training and tactics. In particular Ridgway brought in commanders who were able to adapt and counter successfully North Korean and later Chinese military tactics which were based on infiltrating large forces of men through gaps in American lines and launching surprise attacks on units from the flanks and the rear.

Another boost to the Army's position was General Douglas MacArthur's assumption of command over the theater and his planning and initiation of the successful landing at Inchon. Although taking a significant tactical risk (especially that amphibious landings in that area of Korea could be made) the assault proved to be a spectacular success and largely eliminated the North Korean Armies without having to push them back the length of the peninsula. Within a relatively short time, therefore, the US not only successfully reconstituted the

Main picture: Chinese mortars lay down a barrage on men of the 187th Airborne and their supporting tanks during the advance of the UN forces in May 1951.

Army, but also carried out a very successful operation which appeared to have totally defeated the enemy.

MacArthur's triumph, however, was in a sense too successful. It carried the American Army men to the very border of China and eventually caused Peking to send its own forces across the Yalu river. While the American Army units in Korea were successful against the North Korean forces and eventually acquired the equipment that was more than equal to that supplied by the Soviets, there was no way that the UN armies could hold back the masses of infantry put into the field by the Chinese. Once again American and South Korean forces were pushed down the length of the peninsula. Eventually they were able to hold a defensive line roughly where the prewar boundary stood. The war then dragged on into a stalemate which finally ended in a negotiated ceasefire in 1953. In the last months of the war the Army was locked in a constant battle of attrition against the enemy toward no real military goal. Although MacArthur's boldness can be faulted and his arrogance toward civilian authority condemned, his strategic objective – to destroy the North Korean forces and end the war, made far better sense and use of the American Army then the stalemate Washington allowed to continue into mid-1953.

The lessons of Korea for the Administration and the Army were clear – large ground forces would still be necessary even in the age of nuclear weapons. Moreover it was important that the US divisions be kept as well trained and technologically modern as possible because in the next war they perhaps would not have the time to retrain, rearm, and reorganize as they did in Korea. After the war, however, the US Army again shrank almost to a cadre force as the government put its primary faith in nuclear weapons.

The Army was allowed to decline again after Korea largely because its post-World War II missions had been seen as not to fight in Asia but in Europe. The defense of Europe and the US Army's role in NATO has been without question the most important factor influencing

A typical hilltop fire base in Vietnam. This is Hill 88 in Thua Thien Province seen in January 1969.

the formation of the Army, its units and weaponry since 1945. In February 1950, before the Korean War had even started, the NATO leadership assembled in Lisbon, Portugal for a meeting which turned out to have key implications for years to come. The twelve members of NATO met in a deteriorating situation in which war seemed increasingly likely. Over the preceding five years the Cold War had completely frozen East and West into opposing political and military blocs. The Soviets had detonated their own atomic bomb – to some extent canceling the American 'atomic monopoly'. China had fallen to the communists in October 1949. In Europe, Czechoslovakia had slipped behind the Iron Curtain while France and Italy were beset by internal instability from the political left.

The treaty establishing NATO was signed in 1949 – one year before the Lisbon meeting – but beyond the general structure of the alliance very little had been done to prepare for war. Individually, the armed forces of the NATO countries were totally unprepared for war. Most of the armies were still using World War II

equipment, were undermanned, and had practically no modern air forces. When asked what the Soviet forces would need to march to the Atlantic, Field Marshal Montgomery replied 'shoes'.

The Lisbon conference was supposed to remedy this problem by setting up the new guidelines for building a NATO force capable of defending Europe. The results of the studies prepared for the conference shocked the attending ministers. As a minimum military force, the generals estimated it would take one hundred divisions and over 9000 aircraft to hold the line against the estimated 170 to 180 Soviet divisions thought to be in Eastern Europe poised for an attack.

It soon became clear to American military men that the Lisbon goals were not and could not be met. The countries of Western Europe were still, in 1951, recovering from the ravages of the war and did not have the manpower and especially the economic means to supply the equipment to arm the forces called for in the Lisbon report. The report showed what NATO needed to defend itself but it did not provide the essential answer as to where the countries involved were going to find the means. The inability of the members to come up with conventional manpower and equipment ultimately led NATO planners to look for alternative solutions. This necessity led inevitably to nuclear weapons.

The strategy of nuclear warfare in Europe was based and still remains primarily based on the substitution of firepower for manpower. While the NATO countries could not match the Soviets in the numbers of men in uniform or units, they could bring enough power to bear on the Soviet armies, through nuclear weapons, to offset the hordes of the Russian steam roller.

Indeed, nuclear weapons seemed greatly to

Troopers of the 101st Airborne Division fire from former Viet Cong trenches as they beat off an attack in June 1966.

favor the party – the US Army or another NATO country – that was on the defensive. The Soviets, in order to breach even NATOs weak conventional defense of the early 1950s, would still have to mass their forces and concentrate large numbers of tanks, artillery, and aircraft in a relatively small area to achieve the favorable force ratio (three to one and sometimes as high as six to one in favor of the attacker). Such concentrations, however, could be spotted by reconnaissance and would become the perfect target for nuclear attacks. As far as conventional forces went, NATO only needed a relatively small force in Europe which would act as a trip-wire setting off the nuclear attack. In 1956 NATO formalized the nuclear weapons doctrine calling officially for a tactical nuclear response by the alliance to Soviet aggression at the very start of the war.

NATO's reliance on a tactical nuclear response to Soviet attack in Europe had an important economic effect on how much money the US armed forces, in particular the Army, received in the 1950s. The wholesale adoption of nuclear

weapons as the answer to both strategic and conventional tactical defense needs neatly meshed with Administration plans. The substitution of firepower for manpower allowed President Eisenhower to adopt a 'New Look' defense policy for the United States. Under this plan the US would avoid the costly development and maintenance of a large land army by a reliance on nuclear firepower. Ike was able, therefore, to cut the manpower in the armed forces and keep the defense budget relatively stable.

The European members of NATO were enthusiastic about the nuclear strategy for two reasons. First, with a reliance on nuclear weapons they also did not have to spend money on defense and instead could concentrate their resources on their still shaky postwar economies. Second, and perhaps most importantly, tactical nuclear weaponry and tactical nuclear warfare in Europe were implicitly linked to a larger US strategic nuclear response. Because nuclear weapons would be used at the very start of the war, it was very likely that hostilities would soon move up the ladder of escalation and involve the US and USSR in a strategic nuclear conflict. The Europeans believed that because of the likelihood of this escalation, the Soviets, especially in their weak nuclear position in the 1950s, would be significantly deterred from embarking on an invasion of Western Europe.

This problem of 'linkage' between tactical nuclear weapons and American strategic nuclear forces would later cause considerable disagreements between the US and the rest of the alliance members. In the 1960s the US would try to pull away from the strategy of quick use of nuclear weapons and instead put forward a strategy to fight the war conventionally for as long as possible. Such a strategy, however, would compel the Europeans to build up larger, costly conventional forces. Moreover, it would break the linkage between tactical and strategic nuclear weapons, a deterrent threat which many Europeans counted on as the most important factors restraining the Soviets. For the European members the willingness of the American President to risk New York to save Paris (by threatening the Soviets with a strategic nuclear response if they attacked Western Europe conventionally) was of critical importance. Once the Europeans began to doubt Washington's acceptance of this risk, as evident in the American change of strategy to fight wars in Europe with conventional forces for as long as possible, the Europeans began to look to other means for their security. This issue was probably one of the causes of France's withdrawal from the alliance in the mid 1960s and President de Gaulle's development of a genuinely independent nuclear deterrent, the *force de frappe,* for France.

For the US Army the nuclear battlefield was seen as a significantly different place to operate

The difficulties in detecting elusive Viet Cong or North Vietnamese forces led to the development of a range of sensors which, in updated forms, may prove invaluable in a future war in Europe. Shown here are soldiers of the 1st Cavalry operating a Manpack Personnel Detector-Chemical, more often known as a 'People Sniffer.'

Right: A UH-1 helicopter moves in to a landing zone. While helicopters conferred much greater mobility on troops operating in jungle areas, the comparative shortage of suitable landing zones could be restricting and could present the Viet Cong with opportunities to set booby traps or an ambush.

Opposite: A CH-47A Chinook brings water supplies to a 4th Infantry base camp near Plei Ken Wgo, Central Highlands of Vietnam, 1967. The Chinook remains the Army's standard medium transport helicopter.

Right: A Marine machine gunner and a team mate on patrol near Da Nang in 1968.

Below: A mortar crew of the 1st Cavalry Division fires on suspected Viet Cong positions in the Bong Son area in February 1966.

compared to the battlefields of the past. The effects of nuclear weapons and changes in Army strategy could be seen in how the size of the Army dropped again after Korea from 1.5 million in 1953 to 890,000 by 1959. In 1956, largely as a response to the measures taken by the NATO command, the US Army reorganized its divisions into a new combat structure – the Pentomic division. The new units were specifically designed to fight and survive in a nuclear battlefield of the future wars. The Army dropped the old three regiment structure that was used in World War II and Korea and substituted a division divided into five 'battle groups'. Each battle group was larger than a battalion but smaller than a brigade. Military planners believed that each of these units, operating independently, would be better able to fight and survive in a nuclear war environment especially when they dispersed and maneuvered to avoid destruction by enemy atomic weapons. Each Pentomic division also lost manpower, shrinking to 13,700 men from 15,000. Most importantly, however, each of the new divisions and its battle groups had little real capability to fight conventionally.

But the US expected the next war in Europe to be a nuclear war from the beginning. Conventional fighting power was, therefore, not that important. To provide the nuclear firepower for these new units, the US began deploying a series of tactical nuclear capable weapons to Europe in the 1950s. At the highest end of the yield range, the Air Force began to receive nuclear bombs, which although for tactical use, were still in the high kiloton or even megaton range. In 1953 the Army got its first 280mm cannon capable of firing a nuclear artillery shell. (Unfortunately, these monsters were so large and heavy that they could not travel over most of Europe's roads since they would collapse the bridges.) In 1953 the Army also began to receive its first atomic demolition mines. These devices were designed to destroy strategic passes, create radioactive bottlenecks, and destroy large numbers of attacking enemy units. The mid 1950s also saw the first tactical missile, the Redstone, enter NATO service. Redstone was later replaced by the Sergeant, Honest John and the present day Pershing missiles. Nuclear artillery shells were made progressively smaller during the decade so that by the late 1950s the Army had both eight inch and 155mm nuclear capable howitzers. At the lowest level, the Army also developed the Davy Crocket – a nuclear tipped recoilless rifle round. Thus even a lieutenant at the platoon level could have his finger on a nuclear trigger.

The extreme one sidedness of the US Army's capabilities and strategy in the 1950s toward nuclear war led to a backlash in the early 1960s. Defense planners in the Kennedy Administration, especially Defense Secretary McNamara were shocked to find the degree to which US forces were dependent on nuclear weapons and

Above: Men of the 2nd Marine Division demonstrate their M203 grenade launchers during a joint US-Italian exercise in 1976. The M203 was developed after experience in Vietnam proved that it was far more effective to have a combined rifle/grenade launcher than to have some men armed only with the M79 40mm grenade launcher in use at that time.

Left: A military policeman attached to the 82nd Airborne Division mans an M60 machine gun during the September 1982 Reforger exercise. Reforger is an abbreviation for *R*eturn of *F*orces to *Ger*many. The large-scale reinforcement of US troops in Germany is often rehearsed.

had almost totally lost the capability to carry out conventional warfare. MacNamara's answer to the problem was to force the Army to adopt a 'flexible response' posture that gave equal emphasis in organisation, manning and equipment to conventional and nuclear fighting capabilities.

Flexible response developed in large part because of what the Kennedy Administration saw as the outcome of nuclear war in Europe. The result of following the strategy left behind by the Eisenhower Administration would have been the almost total destruction of Europe. Extensive wargaming exercises, based on the initial widespread use of large and small tactical nuclear weapons, showed that there would be at least 100 million casualties across the continent. All of the population centers and most of the industry would be destroyed. More importantly, the Soviets would still be able to

Right: An M1 Abrams tank at high speed on the test ground.

Below: Reserve Officer Training Corps cadets train on an M551 Sheridan armored vehicle during summer camp.

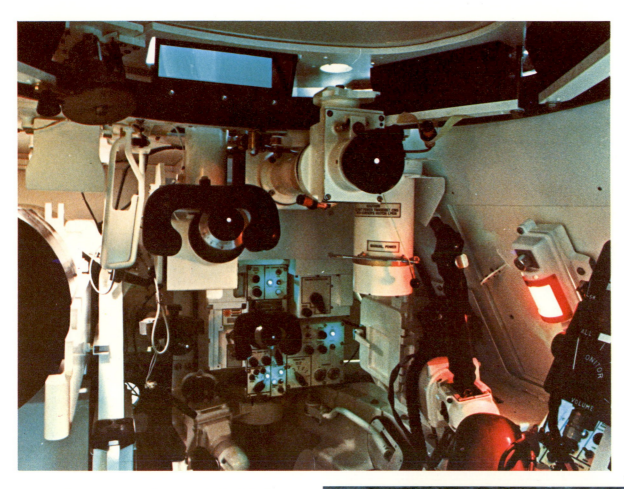

Left: The sighting and ranging equipment in the gunner's position in the turret of the M1 Abrams tank. Modern tank guns are so powerful that the ability to hit targets early in an engagement, preferably with the first round fired, is vital to success in a tank battle.

Above: A TOW-armed M113 APC 'captured' by a Canadian Leopard tank during a joint exercise.

occupy the area, or what was left of it. In any case after such a conflict there would not be much point in trying to liberate a ruined Europe that was highly radioactive.

McNamara's answer to this nightmare was to give the US Army in Europe more of a capability to fight conventionally. The US Army and NATO should not have to rely on tactical nuclear weapons from the beginning of the war or use weapons of so large a yield. Part of the changes took place with the reorganization of the US Army in the early 1960s and the growth of its manpower. By 1962 McNamara had increased the Army to over a million men and increased the number of divisions to sixteen. Each of the divisions also underwent a restructuring. The Pentomic framework was dropped and each of the new units was built around a Re-Organized Army Division. Each ROAD division had over 15,000 men and was organized similarly to the units used during the Korean war. Instead of battle groups, the new division was divided into three brigades. Each of these sub-units was given a greatly enhanced capability in men and improved standards of equipment to help them fight a prolonged conventional engagement with success.

Flexible Response eventually became the official NATO Alliance strategy in 1967. NATO forces would try to fight the Pact armies conventionally for an unspecified time before resorting to nuclear weapons. As part of the efforts to increase NATO's conventional strength the US began to pressure its NATO allies to increase the size of their armed forces in both men and equipment. The Europeans, as might be expected, were lukewarm in their support of Flexible Response both because of the break in linkage between tactical nuclear war in Europe and the American strategic nuclear forces, and the high economic costs of building and maintaining large conventional forces.

Both the American and European plans and good intentions to improve their forces were preempted by events and commitments in Southeast Asia. Washington pumped the money needed for modernization into what turned out to be a futile effort to save South Vietnam. The Europeans without the US taking the lead with its own forces did not follow up with the necessary expansion and improvements. (The Europeans were also afraid throughout the Vietnam conflict that the US would withdraw some of its army and air force

units from NATO to fight in Asia.) At the same time that NATO and the US were failing to modernize, the East European countries and the Soviet Union embarked on a major modernization of both their conventional and nuclear forces. As a result, NATO became weaker in the 1970s and in many ways had to rely on nuclear weapons even more to make up for its conventional forces's inadequacies.

Although South Vietnam was eventually lost, the US Army despite many initial problems and limitations fought surprisingly well in the conflict. This is important to remember because American Army units at the start of the

Above: A prototype of the Light Armored Vehicle ordered by both the Army and Marine Corps in 1982. The vehicle is armed with a 25mm cannon and will be employed in the reconnaissance role.

Second right: Men of the 28th Infantry dismount from their personnel carrier during the Reforger 82 exercises in Germany. The 28th Infantry is normally based at Fort Riley in Kansas.

Right: The XMI prototype demonstrates its hill climbing ability during a test in 1980.

Main picture: An M1 Abrams seen during the 1982 Reforger exercise at Gailsbach, West Germany. This was the first occasion when the M1 was used in field training in Europe.

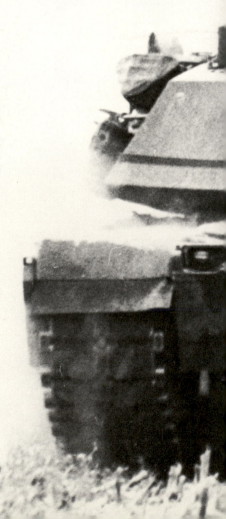

war were designed to fight a mechanized conventional/nuclear conflict in Europe and not a guerrilla war in Asia. The nuclear training of troops did them no good in the rice fields. Armored forces, essential to rapid maneuvers on the plains of Germany, were highly restricted in Vietnam and played a very minor role in the war.

The Army, however, proved itself adaptable to the new situation. The loss of nuclear weapons and armor were more than made up for by the intensive and effective use of all types of artillery ranging from mortars to 175mm howitzers to the 16-inch guns of the battleship *New Jersey*. Probably the most successful US innovation of the war was the development and use of airmobile tactics based on helicopters. American forces eventually launched offensives in which thousands of men were airlifted by helicopters to remote areas to trap the enemy in vertical envelopment operations. Helicopters also played a key role in supply and medevac operations. More importantly, they developed into a kind of flying artillery. While jet aircraft

Main picture: A CH-54A Tarhe 'Flying Crane' helicopter in flight over Vietnam. Some 80 aircraft of this type are in service and are used for such duties as positioning heavy artillery or recovering shot down aircraft.

Opposite: Infantrymen run to their UH-60 Black Hawk troop transport helicopter. The Army now has over 300 Black Hawks in service with production continuing. The Navy also plans to buy SH-60 Sea Hawk variants.

Above: US Marine AH-1T attack helicopters fly similar missions to the US Army's AH-1S Cobras. As well as their antitank missiles and their gun armament, they are to be given a limited air-to-air capability by adding Sidewinder missiles.

Right: Mechanics service the armament of an AH-1S. Also shown is the nose-mounted sight for the TOW missiles. AH-1 helicopters will usually operate in small groups accompanied by scout helicopters which will find targets for the gunships.

flew too fast to lay bombs accurately or near friendly troops, helicopter gunships – like the Cobra – were perfect for such missions and attacking enemy weapon positions and strongpoints.

American Army strategy in Vietnam was simple in theory but difficult to carry out in practice. The generals hoped that they would be able to trap and engage the enemy and then destroy him with superior American ground and air firepower. In the early days of the war this appeared to be the correct strategy. The Viet Cong and, increasingly, North Vietnamese units (as they began to bear more and more of the combat burden on the communist side) assembled into large forces to carry out major attacks on South Vietnamese forces in what appeared to be the classic last stage of guerrilla warfare. In 1965 US Army and Marine forces carried out a series of spoiling attacks which badly mauled enemy main force units – particularly in battles around the Ia Drang Valley. The Viet Cong and NVA forces soon learned from their mistakes, however, and later began to avoid major US Army sweep operations as much as possible. They only confronted American forces when they had to in places where they thought terrain and numbers were on their side.

American Army forces were eventually neutralized by the nature of guerrilla warfare in

Vietnam and the domestic political situation in the United States. In counterinsurgency operations it is essential for government forces to force the enemy to fight. The 'guerrillas' – the VC and NVA – needed to avoid combat and instead wait for the US to tire of the war and withdraw. The communist forces would then move again to the attack. The American Army proved time and time again that it could take and hold any part of Vietnam. It could defeat any enemy force sent against it. The US Army, however, could not remain in South Vietnam indefinitely.

Contrary to the assessments of many observers, the war in Vietnam did not show that the US Army was ineffective or that modern military technology could inevitably be overcome by a determined and patient enemy. Vietnam really had no correspondence to the type of war that would be fought in Europe where most of American military technology was designed to be used. Some lessons were learned and some pieces of American equipment were tested and developed in Vietnam. The Army was wounded psychologically, however, because it was blamed by many for a military defeat and suffered a loss of prestige at home in the minds of the American people. It also suffered because the money spent on Vietnam – 150 billion dollars – could have been spent much better on military modernization. The disillusionment with the military and the expense of the war were mirrored in the decline of the Army's strength (also due to the abolition of the draft and the adoption of an all volunteer Army) from a peak of 1.5 million during the war to 750,000 by 1980.

## The US Army of the 1980s

The Army is now attempting to solve the same problems that have confronted it since 1945. It still is overly oriented toward fighting a nuclear war in Europe. It is still striving to find the right balance between conventional and nuclear forces. It is still trying to modernize and expand to catch up with the Soviets and Warsaw Pact.

The Army in 1982 is still roughly the same as that in the early post-Vietnam years (775,000 with 600,000 reservists). The force is organized around 16 divisions, four armored, six mechanized, four infantry, one airmobile and one airborne, and various other independent brigades and small units. Each armored and mechanized division is composed primarily of tanks and armored personnel carriers designed to fight mobile armored warfare in NATO. The four infantry divisions have lesser amounts of vehicles and lighter equipment and are intended for use in more rugged terrain where armored warfare is more difficult or not possible. The airborne and airmobile divisions rely on air lift capability, in the form of heavy transport aircraft like

Above: A CH-54 helicopter with a personnel carrying pod. Although helicopters are often used in the medical evacuation role the example shown is in fact carrying West Point cadets on a mountain training course.

Left: Close up view of an experimental laser designator mounted on an attack helicopter during tests of the Copperhead guided artillery shells.

Left: Close up of the 30mm Chain Gun mounting on the AH-64 Apache attack helicopter. The Apache will carry some 1200 rounds of ammunition for the gun.

Opposite, top: An AH-64 fires a Hellfire anti-tank missile. The Apache can launch these missiles from cover, lobbing them over intervening terrain to their target, designated by lasers from ground positions or scout helicopters.

Opposite, bottom: One of the prototype Apache helicopters seen with mock-ups of the competing systems used by the pilot and gunner for weapons aiming and flying at night and in poor weather.

the C-5A for long range missions or helicopters for shorter operations, to react quickly and carry out tasks behind enemy lines or to reach problem areas far from the US.

The US Army is deployed primarily in bases in the US and in the major potential problem areas of Europe and to a lesser extent in Korea. The Army currently has over 220,000 men stationed in Europe with 208,000 in West Germany including two mechanized and two armored divisions. The Army also maintains a brigade in West Berlin. Over 32,000 men, in one infantry division and one airborne brigade, are stationed in Korea and Japan. The rest of American Army forces are spread out in 29 forts, commands, and training facilities in the US.

Army units of today are organized in a hierarchical structure based on corps, divisions, brigades, and finally battalions (which are the basic maneuver units of the US Army). There are two corps in Europe made up of two to five divisions each. Each division is composed of three to five brigades and each brigade usually has three to five battalions. Besides each combat battalion, divisions also have specialized units – artillery, engineers, intelligence, communication, air defense, and transport, etc. – that provide essential services that support the front line unit and allow it to function.

US armored divisions normally are composed of six tank battalions and five mechanized battalions. Infantry divisions usually have seven to eight infantry battalions, one tank and one mechanized battalion. Armored divisions have around 325 tanks while mechanized divisions have 270. A tank battalion will have 55 main battle tanks, with 550 to 600 men, organized into three companies. A mechanized battalion normally has 70 armored personnel carriers and 900 men in three companies.

Above: An M110 self-propelled 8-inch howitzer. The dozer blade which can be seen at the rear of the vehicle helps keep the equipment in firing position, counteracting the recoil of the gun.

The number of men in American divisions has steadily grown over the last twenty years largely in response to the needs of new technology and the requirements of operating and fighting with a mechanized force. The size of American divisions today surpasses those of friend and foe alike. While the Pentomic division of the 1950s had only 13,000 men, today's US armored division has 18,300 men. A West German armored division has 17,900 while a Soviet tank division counts only 11,000. An American mechanized division is even larger – 18,500 men – compared to 17,000 for a Bundeswehr unit and 13,000 for a Soviet motorized rifle division.

The difference in manpower between US and Soviet divisions has generated considerable controversy over the merits, capabilities and strategies of the two opposing forces. It is misleading to compare the number of NATO and Pact divisions when the former's divisions are

Above: An M109 self-propelled howitzer with an FAASV support vehicle. Self-propelled guns can only carry a limited ammunition supply and will therefore usually operate in conjunction with specialized ammunition carrying vehicles.

Right: Men of the 320th Artillery prepare to fire their M102 105mm howitzer during a training exercise at Fort Bragg, North Carolina.

fewer but much larger. Critics, however, claim that although they are large, American divisions are no more and perhaps less combat capable than their smaller Soviet counterparts. Most of the excess manpower is in non-fighting logistics personnel. American units thus have a poor tooth to tail (logistics to fighting personnel) ratio compared to the Soviets. In support of their argument the critics also point out that though a Soviet tank division has fewer men than an American armored division, it has more tanks – 335 compared to 325.

In response, supporters of the large American units state that they have a different mission than the Soviets and a different strategy and thus have a different composition and size. Soviet units are designed to advance quickly with little emphasis in the division itself on where logistical support will come from, or where they will get their food, ammunition and fuel when supplies run out. The Soviet command philosophy is to keep sending in fresh divisions as those in the front line are ground down or wear out. American divisions are largely self supporting and would be able to operate effectively in battle for much longer than their Soviet adversaries.

The structure of the Army unit – particularly the use of brigades – is specifically designed to be flexible and allow the division commander to

tailor the make up of his brigades or battalion task forces to the task and terrain confronting him. He does this by adding or subtracting battalions from the various brigades depending on the combat circumstances. For example, a brigade that must fight in the open flat terrain in north/central Germany might be made up almost totally of armored or mechanized battalions. In the area toward the south, Bavaria, the units would be made up of infantry units which fight better in the rugged terrain. Mechanized infantry units provide the swing force for either circumstance. They can either be attached to armored forces and provide ground troops to

Above: An M109A2 self-propelled howitzer. The aluminum hull gives the six-man crew protection from small arms fire and an NBC system can be fitted. A 0.5inch machine gun is carried to give some protection against aircraft and infantry attacks.

Top: An M102 artillery unit attached to the 1st Cavalry Division ready to support a search and destroy operation in Vietnam in 1966.

keep up with fast moving armor, or they can join infantry and add firepower and mobility without getting bogged down in bad terrain.

## The Army, Strategy, Tactics and NATO

The United States Army *Field Manual for Operations* FM 100-5 – the Army's so called 'combat bible' – sets forth the Army's official doctrine on future war and how to fight it. According to the manual . . .

The Army's primary objective is to win the land battle – to fight and win in battles, large or small against whatever foe wherever we may be sent to war. We cannot know when or where the US Army will again be ordered into battle but we must assume the enemy we face will possess weapons generally as effective as our own. And we must calculate that he will have them in greater numbers than we will be able to deploy, at least in the opening stages of a conflict. Because the lethality of modern weapons continues to increase sharply, we can expect very high losses to occur in short periods of time. Therefore, the first battle of our next war could well be the last battle.

Although the Army has different manuals to fight jungle, desert and counterinsurgency warfare, the strategy and tactics set forth in the 1976 edition of FM 100-5 clearly are directed toward the problems of a Warsaw Pact attack on NATO and how American forces will defend themselves. In either offense or defense the key facet of the Army's plans rests on the Combined Arms Teamwork (CAT) approach. Rather than depend on a single arm of the land forces, such as the infantry, the manual stresses time and time again that it will be a combination of arms working in close coordination that will halt an attacking enemy and provide US forces with the means for successful operations.

Armor is the preeminent combat arm in the CAT structure. US Army doctrine holds that the basis of all modern armies – in communist and non-communist nations alike – is the tank. According to FM 100-5, armor is the key to battle for it will enable US forces to blunt and

Left: A TOW missile is fired from a mounting on an M113 personnel carrier.

Below: Firing sequence of the most recent version of the TOW missile with extensible probe for stand-off detonation to improve armor penetrating capability.

destroy enemy armored attacks and attack and break through enemy defenses. All other forces in the CAT are expected to assist and support the forward movement of tanks.

The other CAT members will play important roles in the offense and defense, however. Infantry, whether motorized or on foot, will support the armor by neutralizing enemy infantry positions and infantry-manned antitank weapons. Infantry will also be crucial to holding ground and building strong points to stop expected enemy counter offensives. Artillery will be needed to provide preemptive suppressive fire to destroy enemy forces massed for attacks, to destroy enemy positions prior to our armored and mechanized infantry attack, and to suppress and destroy enemy rockets and artillery. Air support will make a unique contribution to the combined arms team as both an extension of troop mobility and artillery. Aircraft and helicopter gunships will provide key close air support for attacking armor and infantry both at short and long ranges. Helicopters especially will be called upon to transport key weapons, troops and casualties in battle areas and behind enemy lines. Finally, the combined arms teamwork approach also will try to take full advantage of engineers, air defense forces and intelligence and electronic warfare resources.

The manual offers many words of wisdom but places special emphasis on leadership, teamwork, and particularly the initiative of Army officers. The conduct of the war is divided into three areas under their respective commanders. Generals will concentrate the division's forces for battle and set out general battle plans. Colonels will direct the brigades and battalion task forces and control the actual battles. Captains in the companies will direct the individual units and fight the battles. Captains are also given the special responsibility to understand completely the capability and limitations not only of their own weapons but also those of the enemy and how they interact with the terrain. Traditional emphasis is still put on the value of fighting in favorable terrain for both offensive and defensive operations, but other aspects of operations appear to be especially attuned to new weapons and technology and US forces in NATO. For instance, officers are told that a skillful commander will substitute firepower for manpower wherever and whenever possible to save both lives and equipment. He is then told that massive and violent firepower is the chief ingredient to combat power. The key to a successful defense is to detect an enemy's main thrust and then direct forces and especially this massive and violent firepower against it. All of these points have direct bearing on how the US Army is expected to fight and defend in the next

Vulcan anti-aircraft system of the 2nd Armored Cavalry Division in a camouflaged defensive position overlooking the town of Feuchtwangen in West Germany.

Germany to help blunt the enemy advance. The size of the expected Pact attack varies according to the scenario proposed depending largely on how much mobilization (and thus warning to the West) the Soviets want to undertake. The figure of 80 to 100 Pact divisions, spearheaded by the twenty Soviet divisions in East Germany, is most often used. Most experts expect that the Soviet and East German troops would be well equipped and fight very well. Those of Hungary, Czechoslovakia and Poland would fight with a great deal less fervor. Their effectiveness and loyalty might falter if the Pact advance stalled. With Bucharest's break with Moscow in the 1960s it is unlikely that Romanian troops would join in any Pact attack although NATO South would still have to worry about Soviet and Bulgarian attacks on Greece and Turkey.

NATO's military strategy in 1981 still echoes, at least on paper, the defense decisions taken in the early and mid 1960s. Officially, the alliance follows a strategy of Flexible Response and would not immediately meet any Pact attack

Above: A trooper of the 82nd Airborne Division sights his Dragon anti-tank guided missile launcher while his buddy prepares to give covering fire from his rifle or grenade launcher. The Dragon has been in service since the early 70s and carries a 5.4 pound warhead.

Right: Training with the Viper missile, the Army's newest light antitank system. The weapon shown is fitted with a laser attachment so that aiming and firing can be practiced without using expensive missiles.

war in Europe.

The North Atlantic Treaty Organization's land and air forces in Europe are divided into three commands: North, Central, and South. North covers Denmark, Norway, and the Baltic area while South controls forces in Italy, Greece, Turkey and the sea lanes in the Mediterranean. NATO forces in Central Europe, or AFCENT, control all the units in Germany. It is across the plain in north central Germany that NATO expects the main Warsaw Pact attack to come.

To counter that attack, and the smaller expected attacks in the north and south, the Alliance has 66 division equivalents, 3200 aircraft, and 200 airfields. Although de Gaulle withdrew French military forces from the alliance in the late 1960s, most NATO planners expect that if the Pact attacks, NATO could also count on the 50,000 French soldiers stationed in

with nuclear weapons. The strategy is to fight a conventional defensive war to stop or slow down a Pact attack with the forces already in Europe until reinforcements from America could arrive. Although the US and Canada have made plans to reinforce Europe as soon as possible by air and sea, NATO forces would have to fight for anywhere between thirty and ninety days before the first reinforcements would arrive. An examination of Soviet strategy indicates that Pact forces would try to win the war by driving to the Atlantic long before the first reinforcements from the US could have any chance of halting the advance.

NATO planners hope that by trying to defend Germany as far forward as possible, the Soviets would have to mass their forces early on. Thus Moscow would tip its hand as to where the main axis of their attack would be. NATO would then concentrate its firepower and men under the

'Active Forward Defense Plan' to hold the enemy. Under this concept the main fighting would take place in a 50-mile stretch of West Germany next to the East German border. After the Pact forces had crossed the border to attack NATO front lines, other NATO reserves would launch counterattacks against the enemy forces and hold them or at least slow their advance.

A key part of the plan is to channel or lure Pact armored forces into killing grounds favorable to the defense. In such areas NATO strategists plan to position large numbers of antitank weapons, attack helicopters and artillery to destroy the Pact armored spearhead before it could advance very far into West Germany. The relatively large number of man-made obstacles in the FRG, primarily cities, would aid this channeling process. Pact forces, trying to advance as fast as possible, would probably choose to go between and around cities and towns rather than engage in long and costly sieges and street fighting. Because this defense is nonnuclear, a premium is put on NATO's anti-armor forces to be able to destroy a large number of Pact tanks and armored vehicles. Thus NATO has put a great deal more attention on new antiarmor weapons of all kinds in the last ten to fifteen years.

The latest version of FM 100-5, issued in late 1982, offers a surprising alternative to the present military plan and, if fully implemented, will revolutionize both US and NATO strategy for land warfare in Europe. Some American military officers began to question the viability of the Active Defense strategy in the late 1970s. They claim that the chances of stopping a Pact advance with the plan are small. The entire emphasis on 'defense of the forward area' runs counter to all the lessons of past military history which teach that a successful defense is often dependent on offensive operations. They also point out that a forward active defense makes recourse to nuclear weapons very likely because most NATO front line units could be destroyed or bypassed early on.

Although the Alliance would not sanction, at least openly, a preemptive attack on Warsaw Pact forces preparing to attack the West, the new strategy offered by the American officers takes a more offensive posture once the Pact does attack. The new strategy, called Airland, is based on the use of more mobile forces to carry out strong counterattacks into enemy rear areas. According to the FM 100-5 description, Airland doctrine concentrates on:
- indirect approach;
- speed and violence;
- flexibility and reliance on the initiative of junior officers;
- a nonlinear view of battle.

'Airland offensives are rapid violent operations that seek enemy soft spots, remain flexible in shifting the main effort, and exploit success promptly. The attacker creates a fluid situation, maintains the initiative, and destroys the

coherence of enemy defenses.'

While part of NATO's forces would hold back the main enemy forces, other groups of armor and mechanized infantry, using new Abrams tanks and Bradley infantry fighting vehicles, would punch through enemy weak areas to attack the second echelon of Pact forces. These counterattacks, presumably into East Germany and Czechoslovakia, would occur in the first days of the war to a depth of 50 to 100 miles. They would destroy enemy rear services, supplies, communications, command posts and generally disrupt the thrust of the enemy main attack. In contrast to the defensive strategy of

Above: A soldier of the 101st Airborne Division takes aim with his Light Antitank Weapon.

Left: Close up of the simple sighting system of the LAW. Once the rocket has been fired the soldier simply discards the firing tube. The LAW was introduced in the mid-1960s and is long overdue for replacement.

the Active Forward Defense, in its attacks on the main enemy force and its reliance on firepower to destroy an advancing enemy, the Airland strategy depends on mobility and the quick 'indirect blow' to stop the enemy attack and eventually destroy his forces.

While the Airland strategy has a number of advantages that recommend it over the existing NATO strategy, it still has many weaknesses. It works well in theory and computer wargaming models. Existing Pact and NATO forces in the European situation do not, however, assure success for the plan. The main flaw in the idea is the need to hold the Pact main forces back while assembling and launching a counterblow. Many experts doubt that NATO has the air and land power today to hold back the main Pact thrust. The Airland Strategy would weaken NATO front-line forces even more to provide the men and weapons for the counterblow. The Pact might also launch a devastating first surprise attack that would destroy many of the air and land units needed for the Airland attacks before they ever even entered battle. Moreover, what if the Pact forces use tactical nuclear weapons to destroy the NATO forces assembled and advancing for the counterblow? Would NATO forces have enough air support to maintain local air superiority to protect themselves? Such support would have to be maintained deep behind enemy lines in East Germany. If it were not, the counterblow forces would probably be destroyed from the air. Finally, there is mounting evidence that the Soviets have also modified their tactics. They have now apparently developed division sized armored 'operational maneuver groups' to punch behind NATO lines and destroy NATO rear services in advance of the main Soviet thrust. The NATO counterblow forces might have to be used to fight these Soviet forces in West Germany rather than launch the Airland counterattacks. In effect the Soviets would successfully preempt the Airland strategy by launching disrupting blows of their own.

Whether or not NATO adopts the Airland concept or retains the Active Forward Defense strategy, the Alliance will always have the option of resorting to nuclear weapons. Outnumbered in tanks, artillery, aircraft and many other measures of military strength, tactical nuclear weapons still provide the one way for the alliance to reset the balance. Despite some reduction in nuclear weapons, the US still reportedly has between 6000 and 7000 nuclear weapons in Europe attached to NATO. These range in yield from fractional kiloton devices to bombs and missiles with warheads in the megaton range. The weapons are in the form of artillery shells, missile warheads, air-dropped

Opposite: The gunner of a Vulcan air defense system on the lookout for 'enemy' aircraft during an exercise. The gun itself is in most respects similar to the M61 cannon fitted in many USAF aircraft.

Below: A Bradley fighting vehicle at speed on a test range. Two slightly different versions of the Bradley are in production, the IFV, infantry fighting vehicle and the CFV, cavalry fighting vehicle. The Bradley will play an essential part in implementing the Airland strategy.

bombs or air-launched rockets, and torpedoes. Most of the nuclear weapons are with US forces although some are in West German units but under American controls. Both Britain and France also have their own tactical nuclear forces in Europe which could also add to NATO's firepower.

NATO's nuclear weapons presumably would be used to attack major Warsaw Pact troop concentrations or other vital targets. Masses of attacking enemy armor or mechanized infantry units would be the main targets of shorter range systems near the front lines such as nuclear artillery shells and short range missiles. For targets at longer range – such as Pact airfields, command centers, and garrison sites – NATO would probably use strike aircraft like the F-111 or Lance and Pershing missiles. For targets at even longer ranges, such as troop reinforcements and weapons marshaling areas in Eastern Poland and the Western military districts of the Soviet Union, NATO could in future employ the new Pershing II or strategic ground launched cruise missiles.

Even a small scale nuclear exchange with low kiloton weapons would undoubtedly cause major damage to Eastern and Western Europe. From a military standpoint the use of such weapons would also cause additional problems. Large areas of land would be irradiated by

Above: A Stinger missile is fired by Colonel David Green, the Project Management Officer for the system. The Stinger was first issued to US troops in Germany in 1981.

Right: A National Guard tank crew seen during training for reserve units in Germany in 1978. The mobilisation of reserve units from the United States to Europe is one of the most intractable problems faced by the American forces.

ground bursting weapons, cutting off areas to maneuver. To lessen the collateral damage of nuclear weapons, the US offered to build and deploy the enhanced radiation, or neutron, weapons to NATO's nuclear arsenal. These weapons use massive amounts of neutrons to penetrate enemy armor and kill attacking soldiers while causing considerably smaller amounts of damage to buildings and the countryside than regular nuclear weapons. Residual radiation would be minimized and most of the areas would be safe to travel in within a short time after the explosions.

## Weapons

The weapons of the current Army present as much a contrast and evidence of transition as the current attempts to reorient our strategy. The Army presently has a collection of modern and obsolete weapons that give our forces an uneven combat capability. Continuing efforts are being made to introduce new weapons which will be with our armed forces through the next century in whatever strategy is adopted. Such efforts, however, are very expensive and will take years to complete.

The weapons carried by the individual infantryman are modern and growing increasingly lethal. Today's GI carries the M16A1 semi automatic/automatic rifle first introduced in 1964. Although this weapon had some initial problems, these have now been solved and the M16, weighing eight pounds with a cyclical rate of fire of 650-850 rounds per minute, is now considered one of the top combat rifles of the world. For ranges beyond the M16's 450 meters, the Army issues a 7.62mm special match tuned sniper rifle with telescopic scope. The Army has been trying to develop a mass produced sniper rifle to kill at 1000 meters that can be issued in large numbers of the troops. One weapon which the Army has tried to get rid of is the standard Browning .45 caliber sidearm pistol. This automatic pistol has remained virtually unchanged since 1926 and is known for its weight, infamous recoil and inaccuracy beyond 50 meters. So far the Army has failed to come up with an acceptable replacement.

The M26 and M57 series of hand grenades provides soldiers with a wide range of hand thrown explosive power. The spherical or oval shaped grenades weighing around a pound have a kill radius of around 15 meters. In addition to these explosive/shrapnel weapons some soldiers also carry a number of smoke, signal and incendiary grenades. In the future the Army plans to introduce a new hand thrown antiarmor grenade to deal with enemy armored vehicles that penetrate into rear areas despite antitank weapons and missiles. The new stick type grenade, similar to the German potato masher, is supposed to penetrate over six and a half inches of armor.

Army squad level and crew served weapons have changed little over time and have been

retained largely because they are still effective although some improvements have been made and new weapons have been introduced. Most of the changes have come in antitank technology. The M60 light/medium machine gun remains the primary squad level automatic weapon. First introduced in 1959, it weighs 23lbs and can be handled by one man although it is usually accompanied by a two man team. A belt fed weapon, it will fire 500 rounds per minute and in addition to its infantry duties has often been mounted on helicopters and armored personnel carriers. One step up from the M60 is the venerable M2 0.5 inch heavy machine gun. This same gun has been around since the end of World War II (with continuing modifications) and is most often seen on tanks and APCs although a squad version exists. At 84 pounds the M2 is too heavy, with tripod and ammunition, to be handled by a two man crew for long distances. Its 1800 meter

Above and top: Two views of men of the 509th Airborne Battalion Combat Team during an exercise in Italy in 1978. The exercise included a simulated gas attack by the 'Soviet' forces but according to the official press release accompanying these photographs the gas attack was 'totally ineffective.'

A somewhat romantic view of the Army's Chaparral short-range air defense surface-to-air missile system. The missiles operate on the infra-red homing system and are based on the Air Force's Sidewinder. The tracked vehicle which carries the system has good mobility and can carry eight missiles as well as the four on the launch rails. Various improvements to increase the all-weather capability of the missiles are being undertaken. Although Chaparral was originally procured as a stop-gap until the introduction of the Roland system, this proved too expensive and Chaparral is now standard. It usually operates in conjunction with the Vulcan equipment.

range and 500 rounds per minute fire, traveling at 3000 feet per second, gives the squad heavier firepower than it has in the M60.

To improve the firepower of the infantry, the Army has introduced a new light 60mm mortar to replace the 81mm model. The older mortar, used extensively in Vietnam at the squad level, was too heavy to be handled easily in a combat situation. The new M224 weighs only 45lbs (complete with tube, tripod, and base) and can still send rounds to 3.5km – nearly the same range as the old 81mm. In addition to these improvements the new mortar fires special shells that allow the crew to set the round to burst at variable heights above the ground thus increasing lethality.

Since the 1960s the Army has tried to provide the individual soldier or squad with a variety of weapons to deal with the increased threat of enemy armor. The main crew served weapon is the TOW (Tube launched, Optically tracked, Wire guided) missile introduced in 1969. TOW was one of the first antiarmor weapons to use the wire guided system where the operator needs only to keep the sight cross hairs on the target to guide the weapon to the kill. TOW is a two stage missile weighing 45lbs and can destroy any tank or armored vehicle, penetrating 20 inches of armor, at ranges over 3000 meters. It has undergone a number of improvements and has also been mounted on vehicles and helicopters. Just below the TOW in range is the Dragon missile using a similar guidance system. Designed to be used by one man at ranges around 1000 meters, the Dragon has suffered a number of problems and the Army continues to look for a replacement for this weapon.

The LAW (Light Antitank Weapon), provides the individual infantrymen with a light weapon, only five pounds, which can penetrate up to 12 inches of armor at a maximum of 325 meters. The Army wants to replace its current LAW with over 17,000 new man portable Viper antitank missiles. Unguided like the LAW, the Viper will weigh around 9 pounds with a range of 250 meters and be capable of penetrating armor 16 inches thick. Unfortunately, many critics of the Viper point out that the warhead is not effective against the newer generation of laminated armor that will be standard on both Pact and NATO armored vehicles in the coming decades.

Artillery has been the great killer of the battlefield for centuries. Despite advances in other weapons over the last fifty years, over two thirds of battlefield casualties are still caused by artillery fire. Recognizing this factor the US Army has made major efforts to keep this arm of its forces as modern as possible by increasing lethality and range.

The Army basically depends on around 2500 towed and 3500 self-propelled artillery pieces. At one extreme is the M110 8-inch self-propelled howitzer that is now slowly replacing the old inaccurate 175mm howitzers. The M110 has a range of 26 kilometers with regular shells and 30 with the new rocket assisted projectiles (RAP). The M110 crew of 13 can fire one round every two minutes in sustained fire. The tank chassis on which the gun is mounted can carry the 31 ton package across roads at 35mph or across country at 10mph for 325 miles. The other primary US Army self-propelled gun is the 155mm M109 mounted on a tank chassis similar to the M110. The 109 can fire a regular shell 18km or a RAP shell 24km. The six man crew can carry out a sustained fire of one round per minute. Like the M110, the M109 is capable of firing nuclear artillery shells.

The Army's towed artillery is based on one new and one old (but well proven) howitzer. The new M198 155mm towed howitzer is replacing the old M114 155mm gun. It brings a considerable improvement in range, boosting the distance of regular shells to 18km and RAP shells to 30km with a sustained rate of fire of around 20 rounds per hour. The smallest artillery piece is the venerable M102 105mm howitzer that provided excellent service for Army forces in Vietnam. Light, at 3500lbs, the M102 is air transportable and can still fire a conventional shell 11.5km or a RAP shell 15km. Over 1200 of these highly successful and popular artillery pieces have been produced.

In addition to moving toward more self-propelled artillery to keep up with fast moving armor and mechanized forces, the US is making a major effort to improve the lethality of the ordnance delivered. Rocket assisted shells provide longer ranges but even more advanced

Members of an NBC decontamination team practice cleaning an M113 personnel carrier while wearing full protective clothing.

technological improvements will increase the accuracy of shells significantly. The new Copperhead artillery round is designed to home in on a laser reflection on the target directed by an observer or aircraft. Thus ordnance launched miles away will be able to score direct hits with a single shot on armor or hardened positions 'seen' by a forward artillery observer with a laser designator. The Army is also developing 155mm shells carrying 9 antitank or up to 36 anti-personnel mines. Artillery in the future will therefore be able to lay instant mine fields in front of advancing enemy armor or infantry.

American Army air defense weaponry is undergoing a qualitative and quantitative improvement at the squad to division levels by the introduction of three new weapons to replace three older systems. At the squad level, infantry units are already well along into completing the phasing out of the old man-portable Redeye

antiaircraft missile that was first given to units in the mid 1960s. This 30lb missile is housed in a sealed container and fired from the shoulder after the operator obtains an infrared 'fix' on the heat of the enemy aircraft's exhaust. A short range of 3km, high susceptability to electronic countermeasures and flares, and the fact that the missile is a 'revenge weapon' – it is effective only when fired at the tail of the plane after it has passed overhead and made its attack – stimulated the Army's search for a replacement in the 1970s. That replacement is the 35lb man-portable Stinger antiaircraft missile. Although shoulder fired and an infrared seeker, the Stinger is much less vulnerable to countermeasures. It also has a system to determine if the target aircraft is a friend or enemy and can be fired head on toward an attacking aircraft at ranges up to 5km. When procurement is complete in the 1980s, the Army will have over 17,000 Stingers distributed among infantry squads. It also plans to mount Stingers on some of its armored vehicles.

A major air defense weakness for the Army has always existed at the brigade and battalion level where the forces lacked a medium range mobile system that could keep up with and protect attacking forces, supply columns and vulnerable point targets. One solution to the problem was the Vulcan cannon system de-

ployed in 1968. Vulcan uses a radar guided 20mm six barreled 'Gatling gun' weapon mounted on an M113 armored personnel carrier. The gun is capable of firing 1000 to 3000 rounds in short or long bursts at the selection of the gunner. The weapon was seriously handicapped, however, by a short range of 1.6km, and a radar system that only determines range. Because the gunner must see the target and aim the gun manually, the gun could only be used in

Second left: Soldiers prepare to enter a gas chamber as part of their training in chemical warfare precautions.

Below left: A soldier demonstrates an M-29 Field Protective Mask which was recently introduced. Protective clothing must cover every part of the body since many chemical and bacteriological agents can be absorbed through the skin.

Right: A Pershing I missile ready for launch. The Pershing I is 34 feet 6 inches long and has a launch weight of approximately five tons.

Below: A Pershing I missile system moves through a West German village during an exercise. The presence of nuclear-armed weapons like the Pershing often arouses considerable local opposition as well as presenting the Army with many security problems.

firing, the radar continues to search the skies for prey.

In addition to replacing the Vulcan with the Sergeant York, the Army is also preparing to deploy a new air defense missile to succeed the Hawk system for longer range air defense. Various Hawk systems have been in service since 1960 with changes and improvements to the radar, computers and missiles made periodically. The latest version, the improved or I-Hawk, was first deployed in 1972. Hawk missiles are solid fueled, 16 feet long, weigh almost ¾ of a ton (including a 165lb warhead) and are mounted in launchers each having three missiles. I-Hawk missiles reportedly have a range of 35km and can track and engage targets flying in an altitude window as low as 100 and as high as 38,000 feet. Although Hawk's capabilities appear considerable, the system's launchers, exposed radars, and control vans are vulnerable

the daytime and good weather. To replace the Vulcan the Army has ordered over 600 of the new Sergeant York division air defense gun systems. The SY uses two 40mm Swedish designed cannons, each capable of firing 620 rounds per minute of fragmentation, proximity fused, or high explosive cannon shells to up to 3km. The gun is mounted in an armored turret on the chassis of an M48 tank. Unlike the Vulcan's limited radar, the SY's radar/computer guidance and fire control system automatically determine target location, whether it is friendly or hostile, and, if there is more than one target, assigns priority firing against the target that presents the greatest threat. While the gun is

to attack. The new Patriot air defense system supposedly will exceed Hawk's capabilities and be less vulnerable. Patriot missiles are 17 feet long, weigh 1.1 tons and are mounted four to each tracked launcher. Range is probably around 60km with a 200lb warhead. The real improvements in the Patriot system, however, are found in its phased array radar and advanced computer system. A single Patriot radar/computer will be able to monitor and send missiles to engage multiple targets — both airplanes and low flying missiles — simultaneously. Patriot will therefore be able to handle mass saturation attacks. The Army hopes to buy 4,200 Patriot missiles and 100 of the fire control

systems, most of which will be deployed in Europe.

Armor is the area where the US Army is the weakest in numbers of tanks and APCS, performance, and capabilities. At the present time the Army has around 12,000 tanks in three main designs, each of which has undergone some improvement over the years. The M60 main battle tank, weighing 57 tons, was first introduced in the early 1960s. The four man crew has two machine guns and a main 105mm gun with 60 rounds of ammunition. It can travel on roads at 30mph or 12mph across open country. The Army has around 9000 M60s in various bases around the world. The other main battle tank is the 54 ton M-48 which joined units in 1953. It only has a 90mm main gun and about the same speed characteristics as the M60. The Army also has around 400 light Sheridan M551 tanks. These 17 ton machines were designed to be reconnaissance vehicles. Their primary weapon consists of a 152mm Shillelagh rocket launcher/main gun system. The Sheridan has been plagued by constant reliability problems and the Army intends to replace it as soon as possible with a new type of vehicle.

The US currently has no armored vehicle to carry its troops into battle in a manner similar to the Soviet BMP. For troop transport the Army relies on the tracked M113 armored per-sonnel carrier which was not designed for combat. First introduced in 1961 the M113 weighs 12 tons and can carry an 11 man squad 42mph over roads. The M113 has very thin armor and is usually armed only with one 50 cal. machine gun. The vehicle has proved, for all its weaknesses, to be very popular and over 75,000 have been produced in the US and 40 other countries.

The Army intends to make up for its short-comings in armor with the introduction of a new main battle tank and a true infantry combat vehicle in the 1980s. The new tank, the Abrams M1, is already in production with 650 in service at the end of 1982. It has a top speed of 45mph and can go from 0 to 20mph in six seconds — a remarkable achievement for a vehicle weighing 60 tons. Much of that weight is in the use of new laminated armor which supposedly will resist all standard shaped charge antitank weapons used by small man-portable weapons and missiles. The first 3500 Abrams tanks will use the 105mm gun now in the M60 but the last half will use a new 120mm gun (developed by the US and West Germany) said to be capable of penetrating the armor of any existing or projected Soviet tank. With the larger main gun the tank will be able to store only 40 rounds of ammunition in addition to the spare ammunition for its 7.62mm and 0.5 inch machine guns.

Initially the Abrams came under consider-

The Multiple Launch Rocket System fires free flight artillery rockets to give area fire support. The MLRS is currently in low-rate production while research and development work is being completed. Each rocket normally carries a number of conventionally-armed submunitions. A mine scattering system and a guided anti-armor warhead are under consideration.

able criticism. During development its high costs, problems with turbine engines, thrown tracks, and controversy over choice of a main gun made the tank many enemies in the US. Many of the bugs in the Abrams, however, now seem to have been worked out. The Army hopes to replace its M60s and M48s by putting about 7000 Abrams tanks in service by 1991.

The Army is currently deploying the first of its Bradley fighting vehicles (IFV or CFV) designed to carry troops into battle and allow them to keep up with the new tanks. Each Bradley IFV will carry nine soldiers including its three man crew. The passengers will be able to fire 5.65mm automatic weapons from side ports in the vehicle as it moves along. The IFV itself weighs around 25 tons, has a top speed of 42mph, and a range of 300 miles. In addition to the Bushmaster 25mm rapid firing cannon capable of penetrating all Soviet-produced armored

1967 during the war in Vietnam. The Cobras currently use a combination of TOW missiles and 20mm cannons and machine guns to provide a potent antiarmor threat and air attack capabilities. To replace the Cobra the Army plans to introduce the new AH-64 Apache attack helicopter capable of carrying over 2650lbs of ordnance compared to the Cobra's 2000. The ordnance will be divided among 16 antitank Hellfire missiles, 2.75 inch rockets and 30mm shells for the Apache's chin mounted main gun. The real improvement in the new attack helicopter comes in its performance and survival capabilities. Apaches will have a top speed of 200 knots forward and over 45 in reverse. The armor on the craft is designed to withstand 12.7mm heavy machine gun fire and still fly for an hour in addition to suffering multiple hits from Soviet 23mm antiaircraft cannon fire.

The spectacular launch of a Patriot SAM. As well as the performance advantages which Patriot offers, the missile components of the system require no maintenance because the missiles leave the factory already sealed in their launch containers.

personnel carriers the turret has a machine gun and a TOW launcher. The Army hopes eventually to get 6800 of these vehicles to complement the new Abrams tanks.

Because of their great success in Vietnam, the US Army has kept up its capabilities and equipment in helicopters and has plans to improve and expand these forces. The Army still has about 4000 of the UH-1 Huey copters made famous in Southeast Asia. First introduced in 1959 the Huey has a top speed of 110 knots but could realistically carry only a five man troop including its crew. The Army wants to replace the Hueys with the UH-60 Black Hawk transport helicopter that will be able to carry a full eleven man squad and cruise at 145 knots. The Army would like to buy at least 1700 Black Hawks.

The US still has around 1000 Cobra helicopter gunships which were first introduced in

The Army's missile forces in the future will continue to provide the primary means of delivering nuclear weapons over long ranges. At least one new multiple rocket system for conventional tactical support is also being deployed. The Army's Lance missile was first deployed in 1972 and remains the only weapon which can deliver nuclear ordnance (1 to 100 kilotons) at relatively close ranges up to 75km, but still beyond the range of eight inch nuclear artillery. Lance is a solid fuel rocket 20 feet long and 20 inches in diameter weighing a ton and a half and carried on a tracked transporter.

Beyond Lance the Army has the Pershing IA, a two stage solid fuel rocket with a range of 400 miles carrying a nuclear warhead of 60 to 400 kiloton yield. Pershings are controlled directly by the Supreme Allied Commander-Europe (SACEUR) and not local commanders. The Army will try to replace the IA in 1983 with the new Pershing II missile which has increased range and accuracy. With a new second stage the PII can travel over 1000 miles and hit targets in the western Soviet Union. With the new missiles, SACEUR will have a strategic nuclear weapon since the missiles stationed near the border with East Germany could hit Moscow. The radar terrain matching guidance system of the new missile will enable the warhead to destroy point hardened targets such as missile silos. Each of the PIIs will be mobile on a wheeled transporter along with some support vehicles. In time of crisis the missile could be moved and escape preemptive attacks.

In addition to the Pershing the Army is also making preparations for the introduction of the new ground launched cruise missiles into NATO. This weapon, similar to that used by the Navy and Air Force in sea and air launched modes, will be able to travel over long distances and low altitudes and carry nuclear weapons to destroy point targets as far away as the central Soviet Union.

The Army has begun to deploy the first 70 of a planned 270 unguided multiple rocket launcher weapons into its units. The new system consists of a tracked vehicle with a launcher carrying twelve unguided 230mm rockets each with a 30 to 40km range. The entire load of twelve can be 'ripple' launched in less than a minute. Each rocket warhead contains conventional explosive or loads of antitank and antipersonnel mines. The system is designed as an area destruction weapon.

Above: A Pershing II missile, ready for a test launch. A number of the tests of the Pershing II have been failures, adding to the controversy attached to this new weapon.

Left: The US Army currently has no short-range air defense system with all-weather capability. The European designed Roland was evaluated for this role but only a few are being manufactured for service with the Rapid Deployment Force.

# THE NAVY

Previous page: Bow-on view of the carrier *John F. Kennedy* (CV.67) seen at sea in November 1980. On deck are A-7, S-3 and F-14 aircraft of Carrier Air Wing 1.

The United States Navy has traditionally been the guardian of the Pacific and Atlantic coasts, the route by which most strategists and leaders thought the greatest threat to this country would come. Since the beginning of this century and especially since 1945 the Navy has had to assume new roles. Not only is it still responsible for the protection of our shores but has been given responsibility for helping to project American power overseas and to play a key role as part of the strategic nuclear deterrent.

### New Challenges and Changing Roles in the Postwar World

The US Navy ended World War II with over 1900 major surface combatants and 3.4 million sailors and Marines under arms. The peacetime costs of maintaining such a huge fleet – the Navy had over 100 carriers at the end of the war – were far beyond what the US government and citizenry were willing to bear. By 1946 Navy manpower had dropped to 900,000 with many of the ships put into mothballs. But the US did not really need the manpower or ships because she faced no maritime threat. Even with the cutbacks the US still had in active or reserve status fifteen battleships, 35 carriers, 66 escort carriers, and hundreds of destroyers, cruisers and frigates. The only other fleet of any size was that of Britain, a US ally, and the British had begun

to reduce their Navy in the late 1940s because of budget cuts. The Soviet Navy was practically nonexistent, consisting mostly of prewar ships or captured Italian and German vessels, all of which stayed in Soviet coastal waters. The Soviets appeared at this point in time to be putting their primary efforts into submarines, having over 240 of these craft in 1948.

With the beginning of the Korean conflict the Navy was resurrected and grew to a peak strength of 825,000 by 1952. Navy carriers, demonstrating the capability of extending Naval airpower far ashore, played an especially important role in bombing targets in North Korea. Its surface combatants took part in the most successful postwar amphibious operation at Inchon. Within a short time US Navy ships, along with the British naval vessels under UN command, had effectively eliminated what small North Korean navy there was from the war. North Korea was effectively blockaded but the Truman Administration rejected plans to blockade Chinese ports once that country entered the war as a belligerent. Budget and manpower cutbacks after the war again reduced Navy strength, and manpower declined to 617,000 by 1960.

Despite dwindling manpower in the 1950s, this decade still proved to be one in which the US enjoyed unchallenged naval supremacy over the world. With the capability of transporting large numbers of men by air still years in the future, the Navy provided the ships and capability that allowed the US to intervene abroad. It was this supremacy and capability that allowed the US to intervene in Lebanon in 1958 and maintain the isolation of this hemisphere from the military activities of hostile powers.

Like the Army and Air Force, the Navy also underwent fundamental changes because of the advent of the nuclear era. But unlike her sister services the Navy experienced not one but two revolutions. The first involved finding a role for the Navy in strategic nuclear war. Top Navy brass openly challenged the country's over-reliance on nuclear weapons in the famous 'Admirals Revolt' during the 1949 Congressional hearings on the value and efficacy of the Air Force's B-36 bomber. Although unable to compete with the Air Force for preeminence as part of a strategic deterrent in the early years, the Navy begun to incorporate atomic weapons in its forces in the late 1940s. In 1949 the first nuclear weapons were put aboard carriers to be used by Savage bombers. These planes, however, were unarmed and had limited range and it is doubtful that they could have played much of a role in attacking strategic targets in the Soviet Union. They could, however, have been used in a tactical nuclear role for attacks on targets in Europe. Although carriers continue to carry nuclear weapons for their airplanes to this day, their real role in strategic nuclear war has never been very clear. It was not until the late 1950s and the development and deploy-

Below: The nuclear powered attack submarine USS *Bergall* (SSN.667) bursts to the surface. The *Bergall* and her sisters of the *Sturgeon* class carry four torpedo tubes and have a submerged speed of some 30 knots.

Bottom: The non-magnetic ocean minesweeper USS *Inflict* (MSO.456) seen during the clearing of Haiphong harbor, North Vietnam, in 1973. Mines often operate by detecting the magnetic influence of nearby metallic objects.

ment of the first missile firing submarine, the USS *George Washington*, that the Navy got a real strategic nuclear delivery system.

The Soviet reaction to the deployment of nuclear capable carriers in the late 1940s and early 1950s indicates that Moscow at least may well have taken this threat seriously. Lacking a large surface navy to confront the US carrier task forces, the Soviets apparently concentrated on building ships – submarines – that not only could hunt down carriers but also isolate Europe in the event of war. Beginning in the early 1950s the Soviet Navy began a massive diesel submarine building program that resulted in a total of 400 Soviet submarines by 1956 and peaked at 450 in 1960.

The second nuclear revolution experienced by the Navy in the 1950s was in propulsion. Largely through the stubborn efforts of Admiral Hyman Rickover, the Navy acquired not only nuclear powered surface craft but also submarines. The great success and obvious advantages of US nuclear submarines probably were a major stimulus to the Soviets to follow a similar path. The building of the nuclear powered *Nautilus* in 1955 foreshadowed another first – a strategic nuclear weapon system for the Navy. By combining a nuclear submarine, which could stay underwater almost indefinitely and travel for months, with long range ballistic missiles, the Navy developed a weapon that was superior in many ways to those based on land. By providing nuclear power to surface ships, like the carrier *Enterprise*, the Navy freed itself from some of the needs for frequent refueling although the costs of making all ships nuclear powered eventually precluded the building of an all nuclear surface navy.

The value of the aircraft carrier in the Navy began to be questioned in the 1950s because of the threat from submarines and nuclear weapons. Carriers were viewed by many as giant sitting ducks that would be sunk by one nuclear torpedo. It took another war, however, to prove that the carrier did have a vital role to play in war. During the conflict in Vietnam carrier-based planes played an important part in attacks on North Vietnam. Their value came not from any strategic nuclear capability, but from the ability to stay on station off the coasts for long periods of time and carry out conventional bombing attacks on enemy targets. Many in the Navy believe that the service could have done even more in the war to help win it by playing a more active role in mining North Vietnam's harbors and cutting off supplies. The war was costly for the Navy. Although no ships were lost over 200 Navy aviators were killed in combat actions. The intensive use of ships and planes for operations caused them to wear out faster, necessitating their replacement sooner than had been expected. When the keels for replacements should have been laid in the 1970s, the Navy found it was in the midst of a period of high inflation when what money it did

receive would not buy enough new ships.

Many of the Navy's problems in the postwar years, especially since Vietnam, have been due to costs. Probably more than the Army and the Air Force the Navy has suffered because of increases in the price of the weapons it must purchase and the skilled personnel it must employ to run them. Prices of ships have risen from a few 100 million during the 1940s for an aircraft carrier to billions in the 1980s, not including the aircraft. The cost of maintaining jet aircraft vs the prop driven planes of the past has gone up while the 'down time' of the new aircraft has risen because of the many complex systems on board.

All of this is made worse by the fact that not only can the Navy not easily afford the ships it needs but it can no longer get enough men to man the equipment it has. Part of the problem involves the fact that Navy salaries are low and yet it must still attract men to run complex electronic equipment or ships. The Navy currently is short 20,000 petty officers according to some reports. The fact that much of the man-

The *Kitty Hawk* class carrier *Constellation* seen with the support ship *Niagara Falls* in 1978. Some 50 of the carriers 80-plus aircraft can be seen on deck indicating the careful organisation necessary to avoid crowding and confusion when aircraft are being operated.

power, by necessity, is away from the US at sea for many months exacerbates the problem. This causes particular strain in an area where the Navy can least afford to lose men – nuclear ships. Officers specializing in nuclear ships can expect to spend 14 of their first 20 years at sea. The Navy hopes to retain 60% of its officers after their first enlistment is up but in fact now only gets 30 to 40% to stay on. One of the major arguments posed in Congress by officials opposed to building more aircraft carriers, and especially recommissioning old battleships, is that the Navy will not have the men to man them in the near or foreseeable future.

**Strategy in a Nuclear Age**

The US Navy surface fleet has been constantly beset by questions on what role as well as what strategy it will use in a future war. The controversy is especially important because the use of ships and their vulnerability today determines the funding and building programs of expensive vessels far into the next decade if not the twenty-first century. Much of the problem comes down to how the surface fleet will be used. In particular, this centers on the role and future of aircraft carriers which are the basis of the US surface fighting force. It is in a situation involving a superpower conflict that the value of the surface fleets appears to be decreasing.

Unlike the 1950s and early 1960s the US Navy no longer has a monopoly of world seapower. Since the late 1950s and especially after the Cuban Missile crisis of 1962, the Soviets have carried out a large scale naval construction program that has produced both quantitative and qualitative improvements. Their surface navy, although not as large as that of US, now has 290 major surface combatants including two V/STOL (Vertical/Short Take Off and Landing airplane) carriers, two helicopter carriers and a large number of missile equipped cruisers, destroyers and frigates. Recognizing that many of these surface vessels would be vulnerable to quick destruction in a nuclear war, the Soviets clearly still place their main hope of defeating the US Navy at sea on their submarines. The Soviet submarine fleet now includes over 270 diesel and nuclear attack and cruise missile submarines with some, like the Victor, Oscar and Tango classes, superior in many ways to those of the US. Aside from this threat the US Navy, in operations near Europe, will also face attack from the 750 planes – 80 of them supersonic Backfire bombers – of Soviet Naval Aviation units.

It is no wonder then that the value of the surface navy in a nuclear conflict is increasingly questioned. According to US deterrent strategy, the nuclear SSBNs would seek to evade enemy attack submarines and await the order to launch their own SLBMs at the enemy homeland. The attack submarines would in turn make every effort to locate and destroy enemy SSBNs. The surface fleets' main mission

would be to try to survive.

The US has no real strategy for the surface fleet during a strategic nuclear war. If they were in range, carriers might be able to launch some nuclear weapon carrying aircraft to attack the Soviet Union or Eastern Europe. Attacks could also be made with long range cruise missiles from 'new' battleships. The fleet or individual ships might also launch attacks on Soviet ships and naval bases.

Vietnam and Korea showed that the US Navy is capable and competent at fighting in a conventional war with sea and air support to forces on land. However, in the context of a war in Europe, the Navy would be tasked with keeping the sea lanes open and thwarting Soviet submarine efforts to cut the continent off from reinforcements and supplies. While carriers do have various antisubmarine aircraft and other weapons, the best weapon to fight submarines has long been recognized as being another submarine. Thus instead of more aircraft carriers, the US Navy might be better off to build more anti-submarine warfare ships, helicopters and attack submarines.

This does not mean that the aircraft carrier has no role to play in future conflict, only that it may be much more valuable and safe in a non-superpower confrontation. America is more likely to be involved in a future conflict where the Soviets are not involved and where the support of carrier-based aircraft is the difference between success and failure. The British victory in the Falklands war shows the necessity of

carrier air power. The Navy clearly still has an important role to play in power projection and non-superpower conflict where the carrier task force can play an essential role. In situations where gunboat diplomacy is needed the appearance of a carrier task force against a small power can rapidly tip the scale of forces and may even make conflict unnecessary. Carriers are a necessity for carrying out rescue missions such as that attempted to save the American hostages in Tehran. The mobile aircraft carrier provides the means to project US power far inland in almost any part of the world.

Top: The escort USS *McCloy* (DE.1038) takes on oil from the replenishment ship *Savannah*.

Above: The USS *Portsmouth* (SSN.707) is launched from General Dynamics' Groton shipyard. In the background the massive hull of the Trident submarine *Rhode Island*.

Opposite: The first nuclear powered carrier, the USS *Enterprise*.

Right: The *Los Angeles* class attack submarine *City of Corpus Christi* (SSN.705). The *Los Angeles* boats carry four torpedo tubes which can be used to fire missiles as well as conventional torpedoes.

Above: The guided missile frigate USS *Brooke* (FFG.1) at sea in 1978.

## The Fleets

The Navy currently numbers around 550,000 men in over 500 major surface ships, 91 nuclear powered attack submarines and 41 nuclear missile firing submarines. Manpower is divided up with roughly 20,000 men on strategic missions (mostly concerned with submarines) 62,000 with tactical air missions (carriers and naval air stations) 135,000 with support and base functions, and 180,000 with surface warships. By the 1990s the Navy building program could expand the number of surface combatants to over 600 ships. This ambitious program depends on continuous favorable funding by Congress and, more importantly, whether the Navy can come up with the men to man these ships.

The Navy is mainly organized around a fleet system. Each of these fleets is based on a carrier task force with one or two aircraft carriers. In addition to the sailors, the fleets also have various Marine units attached to them. Not all of America's thirteen operating carriers are at sea at one time. One is usually on station while another in the same fleet is in port undergoing repair work and refit/resupply operations.

The carrier makes up the heart of the task force. Its 80 to 100 fighter, attack, ASW and other aircraft are the force's major offensive and defensive capabilities. Of the approximately 90 aircraft on board the USS *Enterprise*, for example, the 40 to 45 attack planes can deliver between 100 and 200 tons (depending on range) of bombs to a target in a single raid. They can also carry nuclear weapons. But the carrier is not the only ship in the task force and is supported by around eight other ships (more if there is more than one carrier). These destroyers, frigates, cruisers and ASW ships are designed to provide additional air, sea and ASW protection for the carrier. Each of the task forces also has two attack submarines attached to it to provide additional long range ASW protection. The emphasis on ASW protection among the ships in the carrier task force correctly recognizes that the greatest threat will probably come from submarine attack.

The Pacific is the responsibility of two fleets each with its own carrier task force. The Seventh Fleet in the western Pacific has two carriers, six attack submarines and 20 major surface combatants. Although relatively small, this fleet has played important roles in the past (providing carriers for the war in Vietnam and the Iranian hostage rescue attempt) and is likely to play an important role in the future if war were to break out in Asia or the Indian Ocean. The Third Fleet, based in Pearl Harbor, is larger and responsible for providing protection for

Hawaii and the coasts of the western United States. It has four carriers (two carrier task forces) 28 submarines and over 60 major surface combatants.

Naval forces in Europe are centered primarily around the Sixth Fleet, which operates in the Mediterranean, and the Middle East Flotilla. Although the smallest US fleet, with two carriers, 14 surface combatants and four attack submarines, the Sixth Fleet plays a particularly key role because of the area it patrols. It has the major responsibility for monitoring Soviet naval activity in the Mediterranean and also to carry out military activities in the volatile Middle East area. The Marine units being used to keep the peace in Lebanon are from the Sixth Fleet. The Middle East Flotilla is composed of two to three combatants, no carriers, and is designed to show the US flag and maintain an American military presence in the important oil transit routes through the Persian Gulf. The largest group of US ships is the Atlantic or Second Fleet. The Second has a total of five aircraft carriers, 60 major surface combatants and 40 attack submarines with a home base in Norfolk, Virginia. Although it does not appear in the news as much as the Pacific fleets or the Mediterranean fleet, the Second Fleet would have the crucial goal in wartime of clearing the sea lanes for the reinforcement of NATO. For that purpose the Navy has concentrated almost half of America's attack submarines in the North Atlantic to counter the large number of Soviet submarines expected to be operating there.

## Ships, Planes, and Weaponry

The US Navy has thirteen aircraft carriers. Four are nuclear powered, eight are oil fueled and one additional oil powered carrier is used only for training. The first nuclear carrier, the USS *Enterprise* was commissioned in 1961. It carries around ninety combat and support aircraft and has four deck elevators. It displaces 89,000 tons, has a complement of 5700, and is 1120 feet long and 133 feet wide. The eight nuclear reactors give the *Enterprise* a 30 plus knot speed and are only refueled once every quarter million miles. In addition to its fighters, *Enterprise* also has three Phalanx gun systems for air defense.

The three other nuclear carriers are *Nimitz* (commissioned in 1975) *Eisenhower* (1977) and the *Vinson* (1982). A fourth carrier in this *Nimitz* class is currently under construction. Each of these carriers displaces 93,000 tons is 1100 feet long and 134 feet wide. They carry around 90 aircraft and helicopters with a complement of over 6000 officers and men. Top speed from the two reactors is thought to be over

The nuclear powered guided missile cruiser USS *Virginia* (CGN.38) carries missile launchers, two 5-inch guns and six torpedo tubes.

The Amphibious Transport Dock USS *Dubuque* (LPD.8) one of a number of *Austin* class Assault Transports which are in service. They can carry 900 troops with their equipment as well as six transport helicopters and from four to twenty landing craft depending on type.

33 knots. With average use these reactors supposedly will last 13 years or one million miles before they need to be refueled. Each of the ships, in addition to their aircraft, also has a combination of Sea Sparrow and Phalanx air defense systems on board.

In addition to the nuclear carriers, the US has eight oil fueled carriers in the *Forrestal* and *Kitty Hawk* classes. The four *Forrestals* (including the *Saratoga, Ranger* and *Independence*) were commissioned in the mid to late 1950s, displace around 78,000 tons and have 85 air-craft. Conceived of in the late 1940s and early 1950s, they were the first postwar carriers specifically designed with jet aircraft in mind. The *Kitty Hawk* class of carriers (including the *Constellation, America* and *John F Kennedy*) followed the *Forrestals* in the 1960s. Each of these ships has a larger deck than the *Forrestals*, carries 89 planes and helicopters and can reach a top speed of 35 knots. They still displace around 82,000 tons and have a complement of over 5000 officers and men, including the air group personnel.

Among the drawbacks to the carriers (especially nuclear powered) not only is their cost (2 to 3 billion dollars each) but also other problems of building and then maintaining them. It took

seven years to build the *Nimitz* compared to four for the *Enterprise*. Future nuclear carriers will probably take even longer. Although nuclear propulsion gives these huge ships almost unlimited cruising range, this advantage is often lost because they still must replenish stocks of jet fuel, ammunition and food. Since most of their escort vessels are oil powered, the entire fleet must periodically stop operations to allow these ships to refuel and restock. All of the carriers in the US fleet will eventually undergo a Service Life Extension Program (or SLEP), reconditioning taking one to two years that will extend their useful life by an extra ten to fifteen years. Even the *Forrestal*, commissioned in 1955, will be in use in the 21st century. Nuclear carriers are especially limited, however, be-

Main picture: The guided missile cruiser USS *Leahy*, name ship of a class of nine cruisers built in the early 1960s.

Bottom: The nuclear powered cruisers *Arkansas* (CGN.41), nearest, and her sister ships *Mississippi* (CGN.40) and *Texas* (CGN.39), farthest, on exercise in the Caribbean in 1981.

cause of their size and nuclear propulsion needs. They can only be serviced at one shipyard, Norfolk, Virginia, which is also the only yard capable of building nuclear carriers.

The US currently has 112 cruisers and destroyers in its fleets. The distinction between these two kinds of ships has become increasingly blurred since World War II as destroyers have grown in size to meet or exceed the tonnage of World War II cruisers. Today's cruisers provide the fleet with antiship, antiair, and antisubmarine capabilities. They range in size from the small 7800 ton *Leahy* class to the 17,350 ton nuclear powered cruiser *Long Beach*. Launched

Above: The guided missile cruiser *Ticonderoga* (CG.47) on her first sea trials in May 1982. The *Ticonderoga* is the first ship to be equipped with the AEGIS air defense system.

Right: The escort ship USS *Barbey* (FF.1088) at sea off the coast of Hawaii. A small but increasing number of the *Barbey*'s sisters in the *Knox* class are assigned to the Naval Reserve Forces, the first modern combat ships so designated.

30 knots. The *Ticonderogas* will have especially enhanced ASW and antiaircraft capabilities to protect the fleet. Antiair weapons included two launchers each for the Standard SAM, two five inch guns, and two Phalanx antiair systems. Antiship missiles include launchers for the Harpoon while ASW weapons consist of launchers for ASROC and Mark 32 ASW torpedoes. *Ticonderoga* will also have a rear deck capable of handling two LAMPS ASW helicopters.

Destroyers in the US fleet have much the same mission as cruisers and range in size from 2800 ton *Sherman* class to the new 7300 ton *Spruance* class. The *Spruance* uses roughly the same propulsion system as the *Ticonderoga* class cruiser, twin shaft gas turbines that give the ship a top speed of 30 knots. Her main armament consists of NATO Sea Sparrow missiles, Harpoon surface to surface missiles, and two five inch guns. The Navy has already launched 31 of these ships since the *Spruance* was commissioned in 1975 and plans to build more if the funds are available.

American cruisers and destroyers have come under considerable criticism from naval experts, both inside and outside the Navy, because of what is seen as a growing lack of armament on the ships in favor of electronic equipment. Critics specifically claim that the new ships, while having improved ASW and air defense

in 1959 the *Long Beach* is a ship of firsts; first US cruiser built since World War II, first nuclear powered surface combatant, and the first ship to depend on missiles for her main armament. The extra room needed for the reactor is evident in the *Long Beach*'s size – 721 feet long and 75 feet wide yet her top speed is still above 30 knots. In the coming decade the *Long Beach* will be modernized to include new Harpoon and Tomahawk missiles.

The newest cruiser in the Navy is the *Ticonderoga* class, displacing about 9100 tons. Each of the four *Ticonderogas* now built or planned are 529 feet long and 55 feet wide (smaller than the *Long Beach* and about half the length of a nuclear carrier) with a crew of 360 officers and men. The twin gas turbine engines (each with 80,000 horsepower) give the ship a top speed of

systems, are increasingly deficient in ship to ship firepower. This is especially the case when an American destroyer, like the *Spruance* is compared to a Soviet counterpart. A Soviet Krivak class destroyer, for example, is armed for four SS-N-14 antiship cruise missiles, two 76mm guns, two 30mm cannon, 2 SA-N-4 antiair missiles, and eight torpedo tubes. All of these are in a ship that was deployed four years before *Spruance*, displaces only 4000 tons, and has a top speed of over 38 knots.

In addition to destroyers and cruisers the Navy also has 86 smaller frigates (about the size of a World War II destroyer) in its fleets. Around 40 more frigates are under construction in order to maintain the present inventory as the older ships are retired. The newest of the frigates is the *Oliver Hazard Perry* class first commis-

sioned in 1977. They will make up the bulk of the new frigates entering the Navy in the coming years. Each *Perry* class ship displaces around 3500 tons is 440 feet long and 43 feet wide and has a crew of 210. A gas turbine engine powers each ship to a top speed of 30 knots. Her armament consists of a single three inch gun, one Phalanx gun system, torpedo tubes and surface to air and ASROC missiles.

The 91 US nuclear attack submarines round out the existing major combatants of the Navy. Their primary mission is to defend surface ships – especially carriers – and to hunt down and destroy enemy SSBNs before they can launch their missiles. Since 1960 the US has only built nuclear powered attack submarines because of their clear superiority in range and endurance essential to this hunter/killer mission. The newest attack submarine is the *Los Angeles* class, often criticized in Naval budget debates because of its high costs – currently around 400 million dollars per boat. Each LA class boat, at 6900 tons submerged and 360 feet long, is smaller than the new Trident SSBNs but is larger than the original Polaris SSBNs built in the late 1950s and early 1960s. The LA class ships can dive exceptionally deep (below 1500 feet) have a speed well in excess of 30 knots, and are much quieter than previous nuclear submarines. They are reportedly fitted with some of the most advanced sonar and computers in the world which can track more than one enemy sub at a time. Their armament consists of antisubmarine and antiship missiles, and probably Tomahawk cruise missiles in the future.

The Navy is also in the process of refurbishing and modernizing three old *Iowa* class battleships. These 51,000 ton ships were used for only seven years in the mid to late 40s. The Navy hopes to use their large guns to make up for some of the deficiency in firepower after having very favorable success with the support given to ground troops during the Vietnam war by the 16-inch guns of the battleship *New Jersey*. In addition to using new rocket assisted projectiles, which will increase the range of their guns, the recommissioned battleships will be armed with Harpoon antiship missiles and Phalanx gun systems. Plans have also been made to put cruise missiles aboard, in effect making these ships strategic weapons systems.

The United States Navy, including the Marines, has the fourth largest air Force in the world – 5500 aircraft – at various bases and on ships around the globe. This includes around 700 fighters, 1000 attack aircraft, and 1200 helicopters, and 150 ASW aircraft. The great variety of planes reflect the many offense and defense missions of the aircraft in power projection and operations with the fleets.

The aircraft carriers depend on three basic kinds of aircraft for their missions: attack, fighter and electronic/ASW. The attack aircraft are primarily the A-4 Skyhawk, A-6 Intruder and the A-7 Corsair which can carry nuclear or conventional weapons. The A-4, now in front-line service only with Marine units, ranks as one of the most successful planes of the postwar

The USS *Oliver Hazard Perry* (FFG.7) seen in the Atlantic in December 1977. The Phalanx gun system was not fitted to the ship at that time. As well as the gun and missile armament the *Perry* class carry two Sea Sprite anti-submarine helicopters.

Right: The Combat Store
Ship USS *Mars* name ship of
a class of seven 16,000 ton
vessels built in the late
1960s. The two transport
helicopters carried can be
seen in their hangar.

Below: The USS *Cochrane*
(DDG 21) one of 23 *Charles
F. Adams* destroyers built in
the late 50s and early 60s.
In the background the USS
*Benjamin Stoddert* and USS
*Rathburne*.

Below: An F-14 Tomcat fighter is prepared for take off on the deck of the USS *Forrestal* in 1972, the F-14's first launch from a carrier. The raised screen behind the aircraft is to protect other aircraft and the flight deck personnel from blast from the engines of the plane being catapulted.

era with almost 3000 produced since the first model was deployed in 1956. The Skyhawk is a one man attack plane with a top speed of 680mph and a combat radius range of 350 miles with two tons of bombs. The Intruder is an all weather attack plane with a two man crew capable of delivering 30 five hundred pound bombs to a combat radius of nearly 800 miles. The A-6 entered service in the Navy in 1963 and there are still 250 in service. The plane has a top speed of 650mph and a ceiling of 42,000 feet. The A-7 Corsair, which replaced the A-4 in the carrier squadrons, first entered service in 1964. The Corsair has a one man crew and an eight ton bomb load. Its top speed is 700mph. With a two ton load of bombs and missiles it has a range of around 750 miles.

Since the early 1960s the Navy has relied on the carrier version of the F-4 Phantom to provide air defense for the fleet. The two man F-4 has a combat radius range of 400 miles and a top speed of Mach 2.2. It can also carry conventional and nuclear weapons on bomb runs in an attack role. To replace the Phantom in the early 1980s in both its attack and fighter roles the Navy is currently deploying around 1400 new F-18 Hornets. The Hornet is a one man fighter with a five hundred mile combat radius range at speeds

Inset, bottom: An F-4J Phantom hooked up to the waist catapult of the nuclear powered carrier *Nimitz*. The F-4J is one of three versions of the Phantom which remain in service in the fighter/attack role with the US Navy.

approaching Mach 2. Its payload can include eight tons of ordnance and Sidewinder missiles for close air support attack missions or a combination of Sparrow and Sidewinder missiles for its fighter role.

Perhaps the most impressive aircraft in the Navy's inventory is the F-14 Tomcat. This two man all weather fighter/intercepter has a 1000 mile range, can approach speeds of Mach 2.5, and attain an altitude of over 60,000 feet. The plane normally has one 20mm cannon and is capable of carrying either Sidewinder or Sparrow air to air missiles. The swing wings are automatically controlled by a computer on board which evaluates altitude and speed to give the wings the best position for optimum aircraft performance. Plans have been initiated to include a television magnification system in the cockpit to identify hostile enemy ships and planes at great distances. The Navy hopes to increase the number of F-14s it has to 850 by 1990.

Although impressive in its performance, the Tomcat gains its lethality primarily from the

sophisticated Phoenix air to air missile system it uses in addition to Sparrows and Sidewinders. The Phoenix, first deployed in 1974, is designed to engage mutliple aircraft and missile targets at low and high altitudes simultaneously to protect ships from saturation attacks. Tests of the missile show that each Phoenix equipped F-14 can successfully engage and destroy four to six enemy targets. The half million dollar each missiles are 13 feet long and 15 inches in diameter, weigh half a ton, and can travel 125 miles at speeds beyond Mach 4. The Phoenix is reported to be especially effective against cruise missiles which make up a large part of the Soviet Navy's air, surface and submarine offensive capabilities.

To help guide the F-14s and other aircraft toward potential hostile ships and aircraft, each carrier also has three to four E-2 Hawkeye radar warning planes. A scaled down and less sophisticated version of the AWACS, the Hawkeye crew of five can use its radar, from a huge radome rotating on top of the aircraft, to determine the location of any surface ship or aircraft within a 240 mile radius of the plane. The plane is able to loiter on station overhead for six hours at a time.

To protect the fleet and individual ships from aircraft and missiles that penetrate these defenses, Navy ships have a combination of surface to air missiles and gun systems mounted on individual ships. For distances up to 30 miles the ships use the Sea Sparrow air defense system; a ship launched variant of the air to air missile also used by many other NATO navies. To replace the old Terrier and Tartar SAMs the Navy is deploying the medium range (10 to 30 miles) Standard surface to air missiles. Standard is a 1000lb solid fuel missile that uses a semi-active radar system to home in on enemy

aircraft. It is part of the new AEGIS air defense system, which the Navy is deploying on the new *Ticonderoga* cruisers, to protect the fleet specifically against low flying cruise missiles. In tests the AEGIS/Standard combination has destroyed missiles in flight and has nearly a 100 percent kill record against a number of different flying targets. Finally, for close in air defense Navy ships have the Phalanx air defense gun system. Phalanx is a combination of sophisticated radar, computers, and the multiple barreled Vulcan 20mm cannon. The system's accuracy is increased by its ability simultaneously to track the target and its own ordnance to make aiming corrections. Firing over 3000 rounds per minute the Phalanx has been able in tests to shoot down cruise missiles and destroy guided 'smart bombs' in flight.

The Navy has gradually moved away from guns to provide antiship capability in favor of long range missiles. The five inch gun is now the largest gun carried on cruisers and destroyers. Even with the recommissioning of the battleships and their 16 inch guns, the fleet will

still have a large gap in firepower especially in situations where ships are required to provide fire support to amphibious landings. Efforts to develop a new eight inch gun have gone on for years with no satisfactory results. The Navy has begun to replace the existing three inch gun on its new destroyers and frigates with a new Italian designed 76mm gun. The Navy claims that this new gun will exceed the old three inchers in performance because it requires fewer crewmen to service it, fires a larger shell farther, and takes up less room on board already crowded smaller ships. The completely automatic system allows this Mark 75 to fire 90 rounds per minute.

Part of the Navy's lack of shipborne antiship firepower will be made up with the continuing deployment of the Harpoon antiship missile. Harpoon is actually a cruise missile capable of high subsonic speeds (about Mach 0.9) with a 60 mile range. Its guidance system enables it to skim only a few feet over the waves to avoid enemy radar detection. Nearing the target, the 12 foot missile is programmed to 'pop up' into a high arc to foil enemy close in air defense systems. The advantages of Harpoon are that not only can it be launched from surface ships but also from aircraft and submerged submarines. The power of its 400lb warhead, designed to penetrate ships first and then explode, was graphically illustrated in 1982 when a Harpoon was mistakenly fired during a NATO exercise in the North Sea and destroyed part of a Danish fishing village.

Opposite: A-7 Corsairs drop bombs on a practice range. The A-7E is presently the standard Navy light attack aircraft but is to be replaced by the F/A-18 Hornet. In addition to its bomb or attack missile load it can also carry Sidewinder AAMs and is fitted with a 20mm M61 cannon system.

Left: A 'dunking' sonar is lowered from an SH-3A Sea King antisubmarine helicopter. The Sea King will also normally carry homing torpedoes to attack any submarines which are detected.

Below: A Sea Sparrow missile is launched from the support ship USS Camden. Although the Sea Sparrow is carried by a number of ships for close air defense, it is in many ways a limited system.

Right: An air controller monitors a radar display aboard the nuclear carrier *Nimitz*. Even in peacetime, air traffic control duties aboard aircraft carriers are impressively complicated.

Below: The Kaman SH-2 antisubmarine helicopter is carried by many US Navy cruisers and destroyers. The Seasprite is regarded as providing only an interim LAMPS system and is to be replaced by the SH-60 SeaHawk. The example shown is an SH-2F Seasprite carrying a Mk-46 torpedo and has magnetic anomaly detection gear streamed behind.

Above: A Harpoon missile is fired from the hydrofoil *High Point* during testing of the missile in 1974.

Right: An old destroyer almost cut in half after being hit by a Harpoon missile during a test in 1975. The Harpoon missile became operational in 1977.

To defend itself against the ever present threat of submarine attack, the Navy has developed a large number of weapons and detection systems. The newest and perhaps most effective of any postwar ASW system is LAMPS (or Light Airborne Multi Purpose System). Basically, LAMPS uses helicopter borne sonar and acoustic sensors to extend the detection and destruction capability of surface ships beyond the immediate area of the fleet. When surface ships detect a suspected submarine at long range, a LAMPS equipped helicopter (usually a Kaman SH-2 Seasprite) flies to the area and investigates with sonar and active and passive sensors. Information on the target is then relayed from the helicopter back to the mother ship where computers evaluate it and determine possible attacks. The helicopter can then be ordered to attack the target with antisubmarine torpedoes or depth charges. The inclusion of LAMPS helicopters even on small frigates indicates the importance and effectiveness of the system in future US Navy antisubmarine warfare.

Close in ASW defense of ships is handled by antisubmarine rockets or ASROC. ASROC is actually a combination of rocket and torpedo (or nuclear depth charge) in an antisubmarine role. When an enemy submarine is detected, a solid fuel rocket boosts the torpedo/depth charge to the general area and then drops it by parachute into the water. The Mark 46 torpedo then homes in on the target and destroys it. The range of the system is around one to five miles.

The ASROC system is similar to the Navy's

SUBROC which instead of being launched from a surface ship, is used by US submarines to destroy other submarines. SUBROC is launched out of the torpedo tube of an attacking sub, breaks the surface and then is carried by rocket propelled booster to the area of the target. It then reenters the water and the homing torpedo seeks out and destroys the enemy submarine. SUBROC has a range of around 35 miles but reportedly cannot be used closer than five miles when armed with its one kiloton nuclear warhead since this has an estimated lethal kill radius against underwater targets of three to five miles.

The last major antisubmarine weapon in the Navy's arsenal is the CAPTOR mine system. CAPTOR is an M-46 antisubmarine torpedo attached to a sophisticated detection and launching system. When deployed, by surface ship, submarine, or dropped by low flying B-52, the one ton CAPTOR sinks to the ocean floor and is activated. It is able to discriminate by passive acoustic monitoring whether a passing vessel is a surface ship (which CAPTOR ignores) or the

intended target submarine. CAPTORs reportedly have the capability of turning themselves on and off, to save energy and monitor suspected peak traffic periods, and may be operational for between six and nine months.

The Navy's submarines have their own inventory of deadly weapons however. In addition to Harpoon missiles and probably Tomahawk long range cruise missiles, attack and nuclear powered missile firing submarines carry conventional and nuclear torpedoes. The Mark 37 introduced in 1967 is an electric powered torpedo with a range of about five miles. It is 11 feet long and carries a warhead that weighs about 1400lbs and uses both active and passive acoustic sensors to home in on its target. By far the most sophisticated torpedo in the Navy's history is the Mark 48 which appeared in its first version in 1972. The 48 weighs 1.5 tons and is 19 feet long. It has a range estimated to be in excess of 30 miles and can reach a speed of 55 knots and dive to a depth of 3000 feet. The torpedo is guided by signals sent through a wire connected to the submarine guidance control unit.

A Tomahawk cruise missile is fired from a launcher installed on the deck of the USS *Merrill* during evaluation of a quadruple box launcher for the missile in 1980.

# THE AIR FORCE

Of all the services making up American military power, the United States Air Force owes its importance, and some would say preeminence, to the advances of technology. The airplane and modern guided missile are, in the history of warfare, very recent developments. During the last eight decades, however, airpower has been combined with other hardware to form such potent weapon systems that it has at times caused experts to state that all other combat weapons, and even warfare itself, are obsolete. Nuclear weapon carrying aircraft brought a new dimension to war not only because of the power and devastation involved but also because of the range of aircraft. The homeland of both friend and foe, no matter how far apart, were the front lines in nuclear war. Moreover, the importance of tactical airpower – the need to gain and hold air superiority over the battlefield – became the key not only to victory but also to avoiding complete destruction.

## The Air Force at War

Two Americans, the Wright Brothers, 'invented' the airplane one cold December day in 1903 at Kitty Hawk, North Carolina. It took the United States decades, however, before the importance of airpower was at last recognized as equal to the Navy and the Army. Indeed, the ancestor of today's Air Force began as a small subsection to the Signals division of the Army in 1907 – a second place status it was forced to endure in one form and name or another for the next 40 years.

It took two world wars and the atomic revolution before airpower was understood for what it could lend to this nation's defense. Despite publicity given to American air volunteers in the Lafeyette Escadrille, formed in 1916 under the command of the French, real American air participation in World War I did not come until almost a year after the US had entered the war. America began the war with less than 100 pilots and 200 aircraft. Few, if any, of the planes were combat worthy. By the end of the war, the air service had expanded to 45 squadrons with 740 combat aircraft (mostly French) at the front. American pilots had a modest but respectable success over the skies of France – 71 became aces (having shot down five or more enemy planes), with a total of 780 enemy planes shot down to 290 American planes lost. Captain Eddie Rickenbacker, leader of the famous Hat-in-the-Ring squadron, became America's top ace with 26 kills to his credit for which he received the Congressional Medal of Honor.

But during World War I the air service played a very minor role compared to the other countries which perhaps was the reason airpower was later given more respect in Europe than

Above: French-built Breguet bombers of the 96th Bombardment Squadron head for German lines to make an attack during 1918.

Right: The identity card of an officer of the Army Air Service during World War I.

Previous page: Two F-15s of Tactical Air Command's 1st Tactical Fighter Wing in flight near their base at Langley, Virginia.

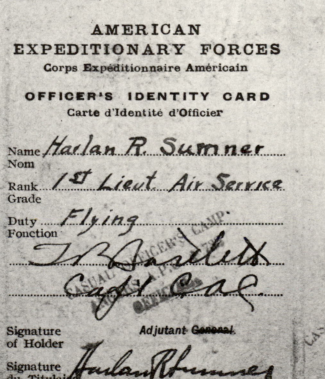

No.

AMERICAN
EXPEDITIONARY FORCES
Corps Expéditionnaire Américain

OFFICER'S IDENTITY CARD
Carte d'Identité d'Officier

Name  Harlan R. Sumner
Nom

Rank  1st Lieut Air Service
Grade

Duty  Flying
Fonction

Adjutant General

Signature
of Holder

Signature  Harlan R. Sumner
du Titulaire

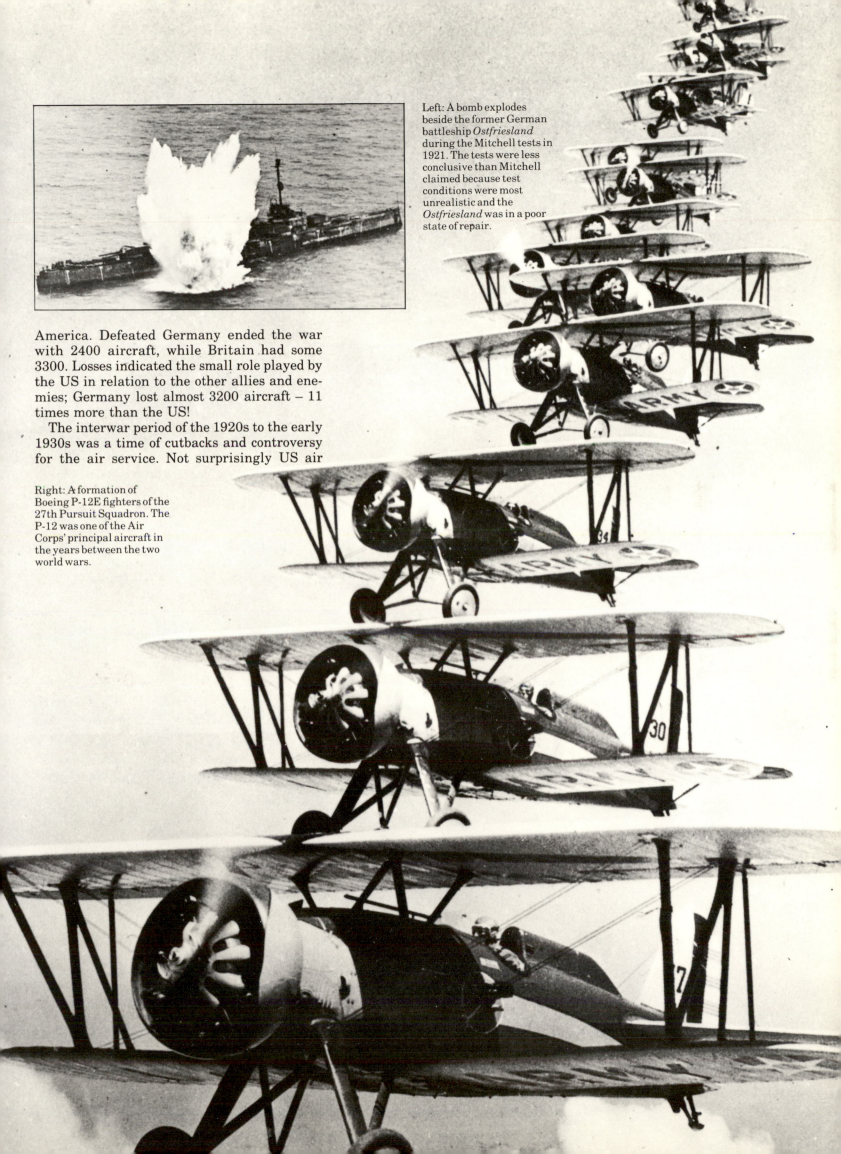

Left: A bomb explodes beside the former German battleship *Ostfriesland* during the Mitchell tests in 1921. The tests were less conclusive than Mitchell claimed because test conditions were most unrealistic and the *Ostfriesland* was in a poor state of repair.

America. Defeated Germany ended the war with 2400 aircraft, while Britain had some 3300. Losses indicated the small role played by the US in relation to the other allies and enemies; Germany lost almost 3200 aircraft – 11 times more than the US!

The interwar period of the 1920s to the early 1930s was a time of cutbacks and controversy for the air service. Not surprisingly US air

Right: A formation of Boeing P-12E fighters of the 27th Pursuit Squadron. The P-12 was one of the Air Corps' principal aircraft in the years between the two world wars.

units, as part of the Army, were reduced in the 1920s as the country and government yearned for a return to normalcy and no unnecessary expenditures on military forces. From a peak of 200,000 men during the war the air service fell to under 10,000 by 1921. Of equal importance was the controversy over the role of airpower, a controversy that seethed around one of the most courageous or insubordinate officers ever produced in this country – General Billy Mitchell. Mitchell contended that airpower would play the main role in winning future wars through the bombing of enemy ground and naval forces. As a way to prove the efficacy of his ideas, Mitchell persuaded the Navy to allow him to test his theories by a practical demonstration. In 1921 a group of bombers under Mitchell's command sunk the German battleship *Ostfriesland* in less than half an hour, shattering the myth of unsinkable ships. But the Army was still reluctant to adopt Mitchell's ideas. In apparent anger he lashed out at the Army after an airship crash, calling the leadership treasonous and incompetent. As a result of his intemperate words Mitchell was court martialed in 1925. He died in 1936, just three years before his ideas began to triumph in the skies over Europe.

Under the prodding of the Roosevelt Administration, the Army Air Corps began slowly to rebuild in the late 1930s and prepare somewhat for the coming war. In 1939 the Air Corps still had only grown to 23,000 men and 1700 planes. By contrast the Luftwaffe was beginning the war with over 5000 aircraft. But if the air force was not expanding rapidly in planes or manpower, it was laying some ground work in the development of new planes that would become critical to the coming struggle. The B-17 Flying Fortress entered production in 1936. The B-24, B-26, P-40, B-25, and P-47 were all being made before the Day of Infamy arrived. And once war in Europe did begin, US air force manpower did pick up so that America entered the war with 6500 aircraft and 150,000 men in 1941.

Two ideas on airpower emerged from the early days of the war that later influenced the US Air Force. First, the importance of commanding the air and air superiority was graphically demonstrated by the Japanese attack on Pearl Harbor and other areas in the Pacific. The key to military success was to be demonstrated again and again in the coming years in battles not only during World War II but later in Korea in the 1950s and the Middle East and Southeast Asia in the 1960s and 1970s. Second, American air strategists fully embraced the idea of using strategic bombing to bring the enemy to his knees. American military planners, following the Administration's decision to defeat Ger-

A P-51D Mustang of the Eighth Air force in flight over England late in World War II. The introduction of the long-range escort versions of the P-51, from December 1943 on, transformed the air war over Europe.

many first, hoped that long range bombing would successfully defeat Germany by destroying its transportation system, industrial base and its fuel production capability. Like the importance of gaining air superiority, the idea of defeating the enemy by long range strategic bombing was also firmly grounded in US air-power doctrine for years to come, but with differing results when put into practice.

The bomber, particularly the long range bomber, thus became the key weapon in American air operations. The first important attack took place five months after Pearl Harbor when 16 B-24s rolled off the pitching deck of an aircraft carrier and bombed Tokyo in the famous Doolittle Raid. The first raid in Europe occurred two months later when 16 B-24s, taking off from North Africa, bombed the Ploesti oil fields in Romania. Germany was bombed for the first time in January 1943 when 53 B-24s hit the Wilhelmshaven navy yards. Most of these raids caused little damage however. The total loss to German armament production in 1943 due to

Above: B-17G Flying Fortresses of the 381st Bombardment Group assemble in formation before a raid.

Left: A B-26 Martin Marauder of the Ninth Air Force bombs a road junction in France in 1944.

Second left: Ground crew work on the engine of a P-40 fighter. The P-40 saw wide service with the USAAF and other allied air forces throughout World War II.

air raids was less than five percent. The really significant raids did not begin until 1944 when in the middle of that year massive attacks by as many as 1000 bombers and fighters from the Eighth Air Force in England crippled some German industries. In the Pacific the massive explosive and incendiary raids did not become effective until early 1945 when General LeMay took command.

Although American and British bombers made continuing efforts throughout the war to destroy German military/industrial production, it is questionable whether these efforts accomplished results commensurate with their costs. Despite fighter escorts, bomber losses were very heavy through 1944. German antiaircraft guns and fighters became very successful at shooting down even escorted bombers and the Luftwaffe often controlled the skies over Germany. In one particularly bad raid over Schweinfurt in 1943, for example, 100 bombers were shot down or otherwise lost out of a total of 230 taking part. The Germans lost only 25 fighters. What was perhaps even more important, however, is that it was evident from the memoirs of Albert Speer, Reichsminister in charge of German war

production, that overall German production actually increased and reached a peak in mid 1944 (three times what it was in 1941) despite intensive Allied bombing. Speer points out, as do postwar studies, that Allied efforts could have been more effective if they had concentrated more on one key area, such as synthetic oil production, and kept this vital good from being produced. Other studies showed that while the bomb and fire raids of General LeMay's planes destroyed large areas of Japanese cities, it was the submarine blockade of the islands that eventually strangled Japanese military armaments production.

P-38 Lightnings of the Fifteenth Air Force during a sweep over Yugoslavia.

Advocates of strategic bombing were quick to point out in their defense after the war that with the advent of nuclear weapons, bombers had the massive firepower that could very quickly destroy entire cities as well as industries. The arguments in favor of the ability of strategic airpower were more valid than ever. These assertions were undoubtedly correct but they were based on two critical assumptions. First, that atomic bombs would be used in all wars of the future. Second, that the target country in question would have strategic targets worthy of bombing and vital to its war efforts.

Although overshadowed by the role played by heavy bombers, the American light bombers and fighter aircraft were important to the tactical air mission of the US air forces in Europe. Fighter aircraft like the P-38 Lightning and especially the P-51 Mustang were crucial to providing the lumbering B-17s, B-24s, and later B-29s in the Pacific with long range fighter support. By 1944 the Ninth Air Force in Europe had grown to over 4000 aircraft. These planes provided close air support to troops after the Normandy invasion and also helped the bombers by carrying out tactical raids on German fighter bases, transport lines and antiaircraft sites.

Despite the mixed results of the strategic bombing program, the air force had considerable accomplishments to its credit by the time peace came in 1945. At its peak strength in 1944, the corps had 2,410,000 men and women in uniform servicing or flying 79,000 military aircraft. Between 1941 and 1945 American aircraft production had jumped dramatically to almost 100,000 in 1944 for a total of 297,000 during the entire war. American bombers dropped 2.150 million tons of bombs, 1.610 million on Europe and half a million on Asian targets. But the costs were high also. Over 65,000 aircraft were lost along with 41,000 American airmen killed and 80,000 wounded.

In the immediate postwar years, the Air Force declined in manpower and equipment like the other services. It probably suffered less than the Army and Navy, however, because of its role as the deliverer of the strategic nuclear deterrent and by its establishment as a third service in 1947. Declining to a postwar low of 305,000 men in that same year, the Air Force then grew in the following years until, by the time war in Korea broke out in 1950, it numbered 411,000, surpassing the Navy. Little of that airpower was in Korea, however, and airplanes had to be moved from Japan and other parts of the Pacific to aid in the war. B-29s were used early in the war in a strategic role to bomb industrial and other strategic targets in North Korea. By the end of 1950, however, the strategic bombing missions came to an end as the bombers ran out of targets. The big prop-driven planes then reverted to interdiction missions against invading North Korean and later Chinese troops and supplies. The weakness of strategic bombing became evident as the bombers were unable to defeat the enemy solely through airpower, espe-

Below: B-26 medium bombers of the 397th Bomb Group in flight over England during World War II.

Bottom: Three F-100 Super Sabre fighters refuel from a KB-50J tanker. The Super Sabre was the first fighter capable of level supersonic flight in standard operational conditions.

Opposite page, inset: A North American F-86 Sabre, the principal American fighter aircraft during the Korean War.

Opposite, main picture: An F-100 Super Sabre takes on fuel from a tanker aircraft. The F-100 was one of the first tactical aircraft to be equipped for aerial refueling.

Left : F-101 Voodoo interceptors in flight. The Voodoo was introduced in 1957 and a number are still in service with air defense units of the Air National Guard although they are very soon to be retired.

cially in a primitive country which lacked essential military targets.

Korea proved important as the first war in which modern jet aircraft engaged in combat, foreshadowing air warfare in the next 30 years. America deployed the excellent F-86 Sabre jet to counter the equally good Soviet MiG-15. American and North Korean pilots fought constantly to gain air superiority over the north especially in the Yalu river valley area which became known as 'MiG Alley'. American tactics, experience – many of its pilots were World War II veterans – and equipment eventually triumphed. Before the war ended in the ceasefire in June 1953, US Air Force pilots had a more than eleven to one kill versus loss ratio against the enemy.

The next combat test for the Air Force occurred again in the skies over Asia, this time in Vietnam. Although a counterinsurgency war, the conflict included many of the challenges of the future and repeated the lessons of the past which the US Air Force sometimes did not live up to or learn from.

Tactical air support, or close air support, of American ground forces in Vietnam was undoubtedly the Air Force's greatest triumph of the war. Time and again Air Force planes were called on to provide close air support bombing missions for American ground forces, especially during the famous sieges around Khe San and Con Thein. Over the eight years from 1964 to 1972 the Air Force dropped enough bombs and other ordnance in South Vietnam to crater an area equivalent to 350,000 acres. The primary USAF aircraft in the tactical air role were the F-4 Phantom and the F-105 Thunderchief (or Thud). At the peak of the war in 1969, the Air Force had a total of 60,000 men and 3000 fixed wing aircraft deployed in Vietnam.

Other planes had to be brought in or developed to meet the special need of the Air Force in Vietnam. It became clear that jet aircraft, because of their speed and inability to loiter over targets, were less effective in the close air support roles then needed. To meet the need for a reliable, slow, less vulnerable aircraft that could still carry heavy payloads, the Air Force brought the World War II vintage prop-driven A-1 Skyraider out of retirement as a tactical bomber to provide close air support. To close the infiltration routes from North Vietnam through the Ho Chi Minh Trail, the Air Force modified C-130 cargo planes and produced the Specter (or

Above: B-36 strategic bombers in production at Fort Worth Texas. The B-36 first flew in 1947.

Spooky and Puff the Magic Dragon) gunships. Each aircraft had four six-barreled 'Gatling gun' type 20mm cannons capable of firing a maximum of 12,000 rounds per minute.

Although the helicopter is often given credit for being the most valuable weapon in the US air arsenal in Vietnam, there were many officers, in the Army as well as the Air Force, who claimed that the B-52 held claim to the title. Detached from the Strategic Air Command, B-52s started supporting ground troops in tactical bombing missions as early as spring 1965. The big bombers were specially modified with internal bomb racks and wing pylons to carry 108 five hundred and seven hundred and fifty lb bombs. (Each 500lb bomb could blast a crater 30 feet in diameter and 5 to 15 feet deep.) Although handicapped at first by having to fly 5500 miles from Guam to bomb targets in the South, the B-52s had special importance because, flying at 50,000 feet, they were invisible and silent to men on the ground. The first indication that the enemy had that he was being bombed by a three plane B-52 cell was when the ground around him suddenly started to explode. By that time it was too late to escape. B-52 raids became crucial to ground force commanders attempting to break up enemy units preparing for attacks. These planes were given credit for having saved the Marine garrison at Khe San in December 1967 by dropping over 53,000 tons of bombs in nearly round the clock missions.

The American Air Force's bombing campaign against North Vietnam – 'Rolling Thunder' – began in March 1965 and continued in various forms after many moratoriums until 1972 and the Christmas Bombing. The main goals of the campaign were to destroy enemy supplies, industrial and military targets, and by exerting 'slow squeeze' to sap his will to carry on the war in the South. The main weapons of the USAF were the F-4 and the F-105 and later the B-52. At first the fighter planes carried only unguided iron bombs but toward the end of the war new

Below: The Douglas Skyraider saw extensive service in Vietnam although the basic design of the aircraft was by that time over 20 years old.

Right: An AC-130 gunship displays its range of side-mounted Gatling-type cannon. The AC-130 version of the Hercules transport was developed for night interdiction missions during the Vietnam War. Although only a limited number of aircraft were so modified they were extensively used in attacks on the Ho Chi Minh Trail.

'smart' or guided bombs entered service. These enabled aircraft to destroy targets, such as bridges, that had taken many missions and lives previously just to damage.

Although the Soviets reportedly helped the North Vietnamese establish and run a sophisticated air defense system around the north and especially Hanoi, the majority of American aircraft were lost to conventional antiaircraft fire. In 1965 the North Vietnamese reportedly doubled their number of antiaircraft guns, mostly 37mm and 57mm guns, to 2000. By 1972 there were over 300 SAM-2 sites in North Vietnam. To avoid the SAM missile sites and find their

Left: A B-52H in flight. The B-52s still in service have been progressively modified with improved electronic equipment for low-level flying and electronic countermeasures.

Below: 750-pound bombs dropped from a B-52 explode on a suspected Viet Cong position.

targets, American aircraft had to fly relatively low attack runs during which they were vulnerable to flak and other antiaircraft fire. Because the approaches to attack the target were often limited and predictable, the North Vietnamese were able to concentrate their antiair resources and set up virtual walls of fire around certain targets.

The American Air Force took maximum advantages of its electronic superiority to defeat many of the North Vietnamese air defenses. SAM-2 missiles were primitive and relatively ineffective, being easy to avoid if detected in time. Out of 180 SAMs launched in 1965, for

A Rockwell OV-10 Bronco close air support and forward air control aircraft in flight over Vietnam. The Bronco was developed for use in Vietnam to guide larger strike aircraft making attacks and help them distinguish between enemy and friendly positions. The Bronco has a light attack capability itself with a weapons load of up to 3600 pounds and four machine guns.

example, only five Air Force and six Navy planes were hit by them. Simple electronic countermeasures, like aluminum chaff scattered throughout the sky, played havoc with enemy radar. Special 'Wild Weasel' aircraft were fitted with Shrike antiradiation missiles specially designed to attack enemy radar sites. EB-66 Destroyer radar aircraft provided pilots with warnings when enemy SAM radars were in use. EC-121 radar planes, forerunners of the AWACS of today, picked up enemy aircraft taking off from bases and passed the information on to American planes enabling them to intercept and destroy the enemy.

The Air Force was also successful in air to air combat but not on the scale achieved earlier in Korea. After 15 years without combat American pilots were rusty or inexperienced in air to air combat tactics. Engagements with older but highly maneuverable North Vietnamese MiG 17s and 21s proved disappointing and losses were unacceptably high in the beginning. To correct the problems, the Air Force began to run exercises in the US to teach its pilots enemy air tactics in mock battles. The results proved successful and the US raised its kill to loss ratio to

Above: The RF-4C version of the Phantom is the USAF's standard tactical reconnaissance aircraft. It is normally unarmed and carries a range of sensor equipment including cameras, infra-red linescan and radar.

Opposite: An RF-101 flies low over the Vietnamese jungle. This reconnaissance version of the Voodoo saw service for most of the Vietnam War but has now been replaced by the RF-4.

Left: Steve Ritchie, the first USAF ace of the Vietnam conflict seen beside his Phantom aircraft at an air base in Thailand.

Opposite: A flight of F-16 Fighting Falcons. The F-16 is one of the most maneuverable fighters in service and can also be used in the attack role with up to 12,000 pounds of bombs.

two to one by the end of the war, downing 137 enemy planes in aerial combat, mostly with Sidewinder air to air missiles.

American B-52s began to launch raids against the North in 1966. The most effective and intensive B-52 attacks, however, took place six years later during the Linebacker II campaign and the bombing of Hanoi in 1972. These operations, which involved as many as 100 bombers during a single day, took place over a period of 11 days. Although aimed at targets in the Hanoi area, they were actually designed to drive the North Vietnamese back to the peace talks in Paris. Thirty-four targets were hit and

## Missions and Commands

The Air Force in the 1980s is attempting to maintain and expand its capabilities in the face of growing threats from potential enemies abroad and increasingly limited resources at home. In 1982 the Air Force had 571,000 men and women in uniform (and an additional 192,000 civilian employees) – not the lowest level of postwar manpower but not the highest either. Over 99,000 of the uniformed personnel are officers including 327 generals. Air Force personnel are stationed at 106 major bases in the US and 43 abroad (with 32 in NATO countries). Worldwide the Air Force operates 2700

Above: An F-106 Delta Dart interceptor. The F-106 has a 20mm M61 cannon and carries air-to-air missiles in an internal weapons bay. The F-106 was introduced in 1959 and some 150 remain in service with regular and National Guard units in the air defense role.

Right: An A-10 Thunderbolt of the UK-based 81st Tactical Fighter Wing ready for take off at a forward airfield in Germany.

almost totally destroyed in 729 sorties that dropped 14,000 tons of bombs. Enemy air defense attacks were intensive during the first days of the operation, launching thousands of SAMs at the B-52s. Fifteen B-52s were lost to enemy action – mostly older models that lacked sophisticated electronic countermeasures.

The cost of the air war in Vietnam was considerable to the Air Force but to say the Air Force failed in its mission is not accurate. Between 1962 and 1973 2257 aircraft (928 Air Force and Navy aircraft over North Vietnam) were lost and the Air Force suffered 5500 killed and wounded. The cost of the lost aircraft alone has been estimated at between 3 and 6 billion dollars. Over 6.1 million tons of explosive were dropped – three times that of World War II and twelve times that in Korea. Although the bombing of the north did not force the enemy to surrender, American airpower was instrumental in defeating the enemy on the ground in South Vietnam. And while the damage done to the North did not stop the enemy, the US Air Force succeeded in penetrating enemy air defenses time and time again and destroying their targets.

installations. It has 72,000 personnel in Europe with 32,000 more in bases in Okinawa and Japan, Korea and the Philippines. These three-quarters of a million soldiers and civilians have responsibility for maintaining and flying over 7000 bombers, fighters, cargo, reconnaissance, training and other aircraft. The average age of airmen is 24 years, that of officers 34, and the planes they fly 13.

The Air Force is divided up into 11 primary commands and a number of other components. Although the other components, concerned with logistics, training and security are important, we will concentrate on the four major commands that carry out essential Air Force responsibilities. Each command illustrates the problems and constraints on the Air Force in the future.

Probably the most important Air Force command is SAC – the Strategic Air Command. SAC has the responsibility for maintaining and, if need be, using two legs of the United States strategic nuclear deterrent in the Triad. The first leg of the SAC's deterrent force is made up of 1053 Minuteman and Titan II Intercontinental Ballistic Missiles (ICBMs) in seven bases in the US. The second leg uses some 436 combat aircraft including under 300 aging B-52 long range bombers, 60 FB-111 medium range bombers and other reconnaissance and command-control and communications aircraft. The USAF also has 640 tanker aircraft many of which are used to refuel SAC's bomber fleet.

SAC officially came into existence in March of 1946. The mission of the command as stated by the Air Force Chief of Staff at that time, has not changed markedly since then:

The Strategic Air Command will be pre-

Above: An F-111D drops Mk 82 practice bombs on a Nevada weapons training range. Four versions of the F-111 tactical aircraft are in service with the USAF, the latest and most improved being the F-111F.

pared to conduct long range offensive operations in any part of the world either independently or in cooperation with land and naval forces; to conduct maximum range reconnaissance over land or sea either independently or in cooperation with land and naval forces; to provide combat units capable of intense and sustained combat employing the latest and most advanced weapons.

In the beginning SAC was small its equipment was largely left over from World War II. In 1946 it had only 37,000 personnel and 270 aircraft, 150 of which were B-29s used during the war. The late 1940s were also a time when the Air Force and SAC tried to avoid budget cuts. During the Korean War SAC sent four B-29 bomber groups to bomb North Korean targets. During three years of combat SACs planes carried out 21,000 sorties and dropped 167,000 tons

of bombs. Air activity against the vulnerable slow flying bombers by Soviet built MiGs, however, pointed out the need for new jet bombers and SAC had to depend on fighter escorts to insure that its bombers could get through to their targets.

The 1950s were a decade of great expansion for the Strategic Air Command and one of revolutionary change. In 1953 the first jet bomber, the medium range B-57, began to replace prop-driven planes and by 1955 the first B-52s began to arrive in SAC units. The 1950s were also important for SAC and the US Air Force, because they marked the period when the first long range missiles were deployed. The early pilotless bombers and cruise missiles, Snark and Navaho, foreshadowed greater things to come. Indeed, in 1956 SAC received its first ballistic missile, the medium range Thor, and two years later these were operationally de-

Above: Cutaway drawing of the General Dynamics F-111E interdiction and strike aircraft. One slightly unusual feature of the F-111 is the side-by-side seating for the two-man crew.

ployed in England. But even this was oversha-dowed by the first Atlas Intercontinental Ballis-tic Missile which became operational in the US in 1959. SAC had entered the missile age.

The Command reached its peak strength in 1960. It had 260,000 personnel, 3000 aircraft, and 46 bases in the US and 20 more overseas. One third of its bomber aircraft were now on 15 minute alert in order to avoid destruction at their airbases by a preemptive Soviet missile attack. Ironically, SAC began to decline in size as its deployment of missiles continued. ICBMs were far cheaper to build and maintain than bombers and less vulnerable. Thus by 1965 and the start of the Vietnam war, SAC's manpower had fallen to 216,000 and 1500 aircraft of which 600 were B-52s and 114 were B-57s (which were being phased out). By contrast the missile forces had grown swiftly in the past five years. From 180 primitive Atlas and Titan I ICBMs in 1960, SAC expanded qualitatively and quantitatively to 821 Minuteman and 59 Titan II missiles in 1965.

Throughout the 1970s and into the 1980s SAC has attempted to modernize its missile forces and keep viable the bomber leg of the Triad. The idea of continuing to have a manned bomber to penetrate enemy airspace began to be in trouble as far back as the early 1960s. The B-70 was cancelled by the Kennedy Adminis-tration because it was considered too expensive to build and, more importantly, it was thought to be obsolete because of the development of advanced Soviet interceptors, radars, and sur-face to air missiles. The B-1 bomber was cancel-led by the Carter Administration nearly two decades later for many of the same reasons in favor of cruise missile development and deploy-ment on existing aircraft. New advances in Stealth, anti-radar technology, and electronics

may give the manned bomber a new life, but the future for this leg of the Triad is still in doubt.

As the last B-52s fall apart due to old age, SAC may in fact be left with only its missile force as part of a 'Diad'. The ICBM part of the strategic nuclear deterrent has also been due for modernization however as the older siloed Minutemen become increasingly vulnerable to a Soviet first strike. The Air Force has de-veloped the new MX, or Peacekeeper missile as a replacement, but Congress has been reluctant to fund the missile because of the unsatisfactory 'Dense Pack' basing mode put forward by the Reagan Administration. It may in fact be im-possible for anyone to come up with a secure basing mode for the system considering the accuracy and power of Soviet missiles. MX may end up, if it is built at all, in old Minuteman silos.

Because of its responsibility for launching a retaliatory strike on the enemy, SAC is closely

Top: An EF-111A electronic warfare aircraft. These are currently under development using former F-111A airframes. Jamming transmitters are carried in the underfuselage fairing and receiver antennae in the pod at the top of the tailplane.

Above: A Grumman OV-1D battlefield surveillance aircraft. The OV-1 can carry a variety of observation equipment including infra-red sensors and sideways-looking airborne radar (SLAR). The OV-1 is normally unarmed.

Opposite: A B-52G moves in to refuel from a KC-135 tanker. Tanker aircraft are often described as 'force multipliers' because their contribution allows combat aircraft to fly longer missions or carry heavier loads to their targets.

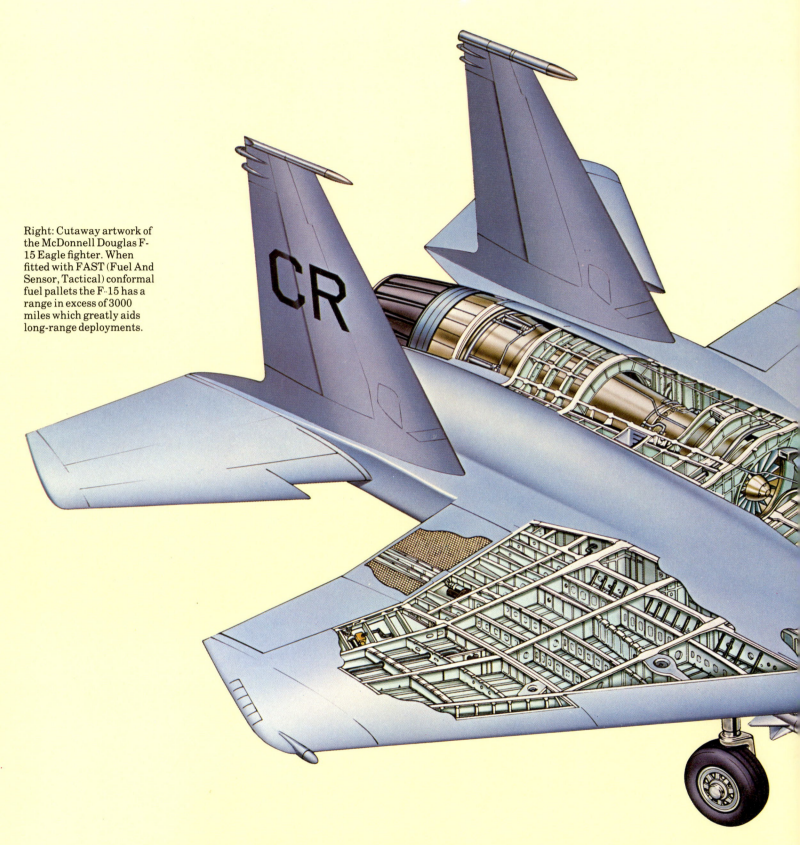

Right: Cutaway artwork of the McDonnell Douglas F-15 Eagle fighter. When fitted with FAST (Fuel And Sensor, Tactical) conformal fuel pallets the F-15 has a range in excess of 3000 miles which greatly aids long-range deployments.

dependent on the operations of another Air Force organization, the North American Aerospace Defense Command or NORAD. Jointly run by the US and Canada, NORAD is directed from an underground command post 1000 feet inside Cheyenne Mountain in Colorado. Its primary mission is the detection and passage of timely warning of all atmospheric and space vehicles threatening the North American continent's airspace. In the 1950s the main emphasis in NORAD was on the detection of a Soviet bomber attack, but with the advent of the space age its focus has increasingly shifted to missiles and satellites.

NORAD depends on the Distant Early Warning (or DEW) line and Pinetree radar systems to provide warning of any aircraft attack from the north. The DEW line was established in the 1950s and consists of 31 radars and 24 stations stretched from Alaska across the northern pro-

Left: The A-7 attack plane has been retired from regular USAF squadrons but remains in service with the Air National Guard and the Navy. The aircraft shown is an A-7K two-seat version used to train National Guard pilots.

Above: Three F-15s and a two-seat trainer (third from camera) in flight over the Grand Canyon.

vinces of Canada. The coverage extends out to 200 miles and up to an altitude of 40,000 feet. The Pinetree line in southern Canadian provinces includes 24 stations. Air Force officials are aware that the systems are badly outdated and have plans to replace some parts with more advanced radar systems. NORAD currently has two over-the-horizon radars (OTH) in Maine capable of detecting aircraft and cruise missiles out to 1800 miles. An additional OTH site is

planned for Washington state.

NORAD uses three systems to detect possible Soviet intercontinental ballistic missile attacks. The first line of defense is a number of surveilance satellites positioned constantly in geosynchronous orbits which can detect missile launches 90 seconds after blast off. The main radar detection system is the Ballistic Missile Early Warning System or BMEWS established in the early 1960s. BMEWS has 12 huge radars

at three stations in Alaska, Greenland and England, to provide ICBM and IRBM detection out to 3000 miles. As the threat of sneak attack from Soviet missile submarines in the Pacific and Atlantic grew in the 1960s, the Air Force responded with the deployment of two phased array radar systems at California and Massachusetts to detect SLBMs to a range of 3300 miles. NORAD also has one radar in Florida to detect launches from the Caribbean and warheads coming over the south pole in a fractional orbit bombardment path. Realistically, NORAD could probably give 20 to 30 minutes warning of an ICBM attack and 5 to 10 minutes of an SLBM launch.

One section of NORAD that has steadily grown in importance over the past dozen years is the Space Defense Operations Center (or SPACDOC) which has responsibility for keeping track of objects and satellites in orbit. Not

A C-5 Galaxy transport of Military Airlift Command at a base in Alaska. Typical performance figures for the C-5 would give a range of 6500 miles with a 40-ton payload. Maximum payload is 220,000 pounds.

Above: An SR-71 Blackbird strategic reconnaissance aircraft in flight near Beale AFB, California. Many aspects of the Blackbird are classified but it can attain speeds over Mach 3 and its operating altitude is between 80,000 and 100,000 feet. Much of the aircraft is constructed of titanium and the Blackbird uses special JP-7 high temperature fuel.

Opposite: An RC-135 electronic intelligence gathering aircraft. A number of different versions of this aircraft are in service with a variety of aerials and antennae whose precise functions have never been publicly explained but will presumably include active radar and radio and radar detection.

only does SPACDOC monitor the path of Soviet, American and other nations satellites, but also all the other space junk (burned out boosters and dead satellites, etc.) that are in orbit for a total of 5000 different objects. NORAD has both radar and optical tracking systems in Turkey, California, Canada, New Mexico, South Korea, Italy, Hawaii and New Zealand which constantly send information on space activity to SPAC-DOC headquarters in Colorado. These radars reportedly can detect an object one foot in diameter 2000 miles in space while the optical cameras can 'see' the same sized object (in good weather with reflected light) 2500 miles out in space.

In general NORAD's missile detection system is fairly effective. Despite periodic news reports of computer chip failures causing false alerts to be sent to SAC, NORAD capabilities with the addition of new radars and computers have increased in reliability and effectiveness over the systems of the past. The ability to monitor aircraft, however, has deteriorated over the past years. The argument can be made that resources would be wasted on this because the Soviets have let their manned bomber force decline. If the Soviets were to build a new bomber, however, the US would be hard pressed not only to detect such aircraft but also to defend the 1000s of miles of North American airspace since the Tactical Air Command, responsible for air defense, has less than three hundred fighters and no long range surface to air missiles. Although NORAD could alert the Strategic Air

Command to an enemy missile atack, there is nothing the US could do to defend itself directly against it. The US dismantled its one ABM site in North Dakota in 1976 although it still operates the phased array radar at this site. As part of an effort to protect American satellites in orbit, the Air Force is developing a new ASAT interceptor missile which will be launched from high altitude by an F-15 fighter.

Next to SAC and NORAD, the most important Air Force command is probably the United States Air Forces in Europe, or USAFE. USAFE has the mission of providing air support – with both conventional and nuclear weapons – to US and NATO forces in Europe. The combined NATO air forces have the responsibility for covering over 7,000,000 square miles in Europe. To do its share USAFE has 57,000 servicemen on the continent with the largest contingent, 22,000, in England. The command has around 700 combat aircraft. The main deployments are in England, with about 300 F-111s, A-10s and F-4s, in Germany with about 280 F-16s, F-4s and F-15s, and the rest primarily in Spain, Iceland, and the Netherlands. USAFE uses 29 airfields in these five countries in addition to bases in Italy, Greece and Turkey.

In theory, the close air support mission of USAFE depends on achieving three goals in sequence. First the air forces are supposed to gain air superiority, hopefully across all of the theater, but at least over the main battle area. This means that enemy aircraft will have to be destroyed in the air and on the ground at their

Above: A KC-10 Extender tanker aircraft. This version of the DC-10 airliner is currently entering service. A total of 60 may eventually be procured.

Right: Technicians service the APQ-120 radar of an F-4E Phantom.

bases (preferably the latter where they are more vulnerable and massed). In addition to the destruction of enemy aircraft, however, air forces will also have to destroy enemy air defense systems in order to insure free access for friendly aircraft over the battlefield. Once this is accomplished, the air force will move into the second goal of disrupting and interdicting the supplies and rear services of the enemy ground forces. They will also have to attack and destroy enemy efforts to reinforce areas with men and equipment. Finally, close air support aircraft will have to aid the attack of the mechanized ground forces by striking enemy front line units, particularly armor and artillery and command-control-communications ($C^3$) targets.

In practice USAFE's close air support mission in Europe presents some great problems especially considering the build up of Warsaw Pact air forces in the last decade. Pact forces now outnumber NATO air forces in ground support, fighter and interceptor aircraft by 6700 to 3100. Because of the distances involved it is much more likely that the commander of the Pact air forces will be better able to bring in reinforcement aircraft from the Soviet Union than the USAFE commander will be able to get more planes from the US and Canada. With the present NATO strategy of Active Forward Defense, it is highly likely that Pact forces will strike the first blow. It will be their side that attempts to destroy NATO and USAFE aircraft at their bases. Thus, facing an attacking enemy, the most likely objective for USAFE will not be to gain air superiority over the other side's territory but to maintain it over West Germany. For this they will need to carry out three somewhat different close air support missions than those mentioned above which will each be of critical importance. First, their aircraft, particularly the A-10s which were specially designed for this purpose, will have to attack and destroy advancing enemy armor. Second, they will have to keep enough aircraft flying to be able to carry out nuclear strike on enemy forces. Finally, they will have constantly to challenge Pact attempts to gain air superiority over local battle areas to prevent NATO ground units from being cut off and annihilated.

Without striking the enemy first, the tasks of USAFE under the Airland doctrine would be even more difficult. Assuming that the enemy has already begun his attack, NATO forces, using the Airland strategy, would be preparing to launch counterattacks through weak points into the enemy rear areas. USAFE would have to provide the air cover for attacking NATO forces. Thus, in addition to keeping the practical goals mentioned above, strained USAFE formations would also have to try to achieve the theoretical objectives.

The Air Force's Military Airlift Command is the third important command and is likely to grow in size and importance in the future. Currently MAC has 72,000 men and flies out of 13 home bases in the US and uses 300 bases in 24 countries. It has around 1000 aircraft, most of which are cargo planes. The bulk of the craft and lifting power are concentrated in 259 C-130s, 241 C-141s, and 77 C-5As. To augment its lift capability in time of crisis, MAC could also take over a large number of civilian airline and cargo aircraft in the US.

The Military Airlift Command will grow in importance because it is the primary means the US has to project power quickly to areas very distant from the United States. With its cargo aircraft, MAC has the capability to transport airborne troops and equipment to any part of the world. In the future it will probably be used to carry out support and resupply mission in three scenarios. First and foremost it will be used to transport American reinforcements to Europe in case of Soviet attack. Even with large numbers of extra civilian aircraft commandeered into service, reinforcing NATO by air would be a dangerous undertaking because of potential Pact air attacks. Second, MAC would also be responsible for rushing Marine units or other forces into trouble spots as part of the Rapid Deployment Forces. This mission would be especially difficult – if not impossible – if war was going on in Europe at the same time with aircraft and men badly needed elsewhere. Finally, MAC may also be needed to resupply American allies quickly. The crucial political and military role played by American cargo aircraft during the 1973 Arab-Israeli war was very evident and is likely to be repeated.

## Wings and Talons

The Air Force relies on many new and old aircraft and weapons to carry out its non-combat and combat missions. Like the other services, it is in the midst of a period when the next generation of equipment is replacing current models.

The Air Force's fighter aircraft are used primarily for air defense and air superiority missions but in the course of any model's operational lifetime it is usually fitted with extra bomb racks for close air support. A good example of this is the F-4 Phantom which first joined Air Force units in 1963 and was the mainstay of Air Force operations in Vietnam. Like the Navy and Marines, the Air Force used the Phantom to carry bombs for close air support missions but also to fly air superiority missions over the North, guarding the slower F-105s and later B-52s. The F-4 is a two-man fighter with a pilot and radar/weapons officer, with a top speed of Mach 2.2, a ceiling of 70,000 feet, and a combat radius of 600 miles. The plane can carry eight tons of rockets, bombs and missiles in addition to Sparrow and Sidewinder air to air missiles. In 1976 the Air Force had nearly 1100 F-4s but that number has now dropped as the aircraft is currently being phased out and replaced.

The Air Force has around 100 F-5 Tigers, also known as the Freedom Fighter. The Tiger is used by the Air Force for training and has been

A C-141A and a C-141B Starlifter. All C-141s in service with the USAF have been modified to C-141B standard by 'stretching' the fuselage by some 23 feet giving a considerable increase in cargo capacity.

a very successful export to Third World countries with well over a thousand planes sold abroad. Carrying only a pilot, the F-5 has a top speed of around Mach 1.6 and a ceiling of around 52,000 feet. It will take 7000lbs of ordnance including two Sidewinder missiles and two 20mm cannons. Because of its resemblance to the MiG-21, the Tiger has a unique role in the US Air Force. It is used in the Aggressor Squadrons at Nellis Air Force base in Nevada to simulate Soviet air attacks. These 'Red Flag' exercises provide important training for Air Force pilots by giving them experience as close as possible to real combat against aircraft resemb-

Below: An F-16 fires a Maverick missile. The Maverick can be fired from many different aircraft types.

Bottom: An F-5E Aggressor used in the Red Flag program of Dissimilar Air Combat Training. The F-5s used in this program are painted in typical Soviet camouflage and are operated within a strict ground control system after Soviet practice.

ling and using tactics like those of Warsaw Pact countries.

The Phantom is slowly being replaced by the new McDonnell Douglas F-15 Eagle, a very advanced, but very expensive, air superiority fighter. First deployed in 1977, the Eagle is the American answer to the latest generation of fighters introduced in the 1970s by the Soviet Union, particularly the MiG-25. The all weather Eagle is a single seat aircraft with a top speed of more than Mach 2.5 and a ceiling of over 100,000 feet. With its two powerful engines the Eagle holds over eight acceleration to height records including going from take-off to 65,000

feet in two minutes. The Eagle will carry a 16,000lb load, including four Sidewinder and four Sparrow missiles in addition to a 20mm Gatling gun type cannon. The Air Force had over 600 Eagles in 1982 and wants to increase the inventory to 1100.

Because of the Eagle's high cost, around 20 million dollars each, the Air Force began in the mid 1970s to look for a slightly less capable but cheaper fighter to fill the needs where the US could not afford to deploy F-15s. The result was the development of the F-16 Fighting Falcon – a cheaper and in some ways better aircraft than the F-15. Although slower at Mach 2 than the F-4 and F-15, the F-16 is smaller (harder to see or detect on radar) much more maneuverable (with excellent pilot visibility) and at 12,000lbs unloaded weighs less than half as much as a Phantom. For its air defense role the Falcon has a 20mm cannon and two Sidewinder missiles. At around a third to half the cost of an Eagle, the F-16 will probably take over many of the air defense roles given to the F-4. The first Falcon became operational in 1979. Around 300 are now in service and the Air Force hopes to increase this number to 2300.

The Air Force has two other aircraft which are primarily designed for a ground support role. The older of the two is the F-111 first deployed to Air Force units in 1967. The F-111

carries a two-man crew at speeds up to Mach 2.5 with a 31,000lb bomb load. The variable-geometry swing wing allows the pilot to dash at high speeds at high altitudes or use terrain hugging radar to skim at a few hundred feet off the ground to avoid enemy radar. The plane was used in bombing missions during the Vietnam war but experienced problems when the terrain following radar and computers malfunctioned, causing crashes. The 200 F-111s in NATO would probably be used to carry nuclear weapons on deep strike missions behind Pact lines.

As a result of the needs that became evident during the Vietnam war for a true close air support aircraft, the Air Force developed and deployed the A-10 Thunderbolt. Although it only has a top speed of 490mph (even less when carrying a full load) the A-10 can carry eight tons of bombs and rockets. To protect him from the enemy ground fire, the pilot of the A-10 is protected by special titanium armor capable of resisting 23mm cannon fire. The Thunderbolt's two engines are positioned above the main fuselage to minimize susceptability to detection and damage from infrared antiaircraft missiles. In addition to the tons of bombs and rockets it carries on wing pylons, the Thunderbolt has been given a key role in anti-armor defense with a unique weapon. It carries a 30mm cannon capable of firing 2200-4000 rounds per minute of depleted uranium shells (for extra mass and power) that can penetrate the armor on most enemy tanks.

Despite its attention to battlefield survivability, there is considerable controversy in the Air Force over whether the Thunderbolt (actually called the Warthog by its pilots) will be able to withstand the intense groundfire expected from Pact units in the 1980s. The Air Force now has 330 A-10s and originally wanted 400 more. There is now doubt that this many Thunderbolts will be produced.

Transport and tanker aircraft make up a crucial, but often overlooked, part of the Air Force flying machine inventory because of the role they play in power projection and refueling front line fighters and bombers. The largest

Top: A C-130E Hercules transport aircraft of the 36th Tactical Airlift Squadron in flight over Mount St. Helens in 1978.

Above: An AGM-88A High-speed Anti-Radiation Missile (HARM) mounted on an F-4G Wild Weasel aircraft. Specialized Wild Weasel or defense suppression aircraft were developed during the Vietnam War. They employ missiles like the HARM to attack radar and missile sites.

Above: Two A-7Ds with
their ventral dive brakes
extended. They are armed
with Mk 82 500-pound
bombs.

transport is the much maligned C-5A Galaxy. Since the initial deployment in 1969, and the overcoming of early problems with the landing gear, the Air Force has acquired 80 of these giants. Each Galaxy can lift 205,000lbs or the equivalent of two medium tanks or three helicopters. In addition to the crew of five it can carry 350 combat troops. With a seventy-ton load the C-5 has a range of 3500 miles. Top speed unloaded is 580mph.

Completing the inventory of primary cargo aircraft, the Air Force also has around 600 C-141s and C-130 transports. The C-141 Starlifter joined Air Force units in 1965 and can carry 90,000lbs at ranges up to 3000 miles at a top speed of 560mph. The C-130 Hercules was first delivered in 1956 but its reliability and utility made it an Air Force workhorse in many airlift operations. Each prop-driven C-130 can carry 80 troops or 15,000lbs 2100 miles at 380mph.

The Air Force provides in-flight refueling to its SAC aircraft as well as fighters through over 600 KC-135 stratotankers. The KC-135 is a commercial Boeing 707 airframe, modified in-

Left: Cutaway artwork of the C-5 Galaxy transport aircraft.

Above: Loading a Roland surface-to-air missile system aboard a Galaxy transport. The Roland was evaluated by the US Army but found to be too expensive and only a few systems are in service.

ternally with fuel tanks and refueling equipment. Each plane can carry a maximum of 120,000lbs of fuel to a range of 1200 miles. In order to augment the aging tanker fleet, the Air Force has begun to deploy new KC-10A Extenders based on the commercial DC-10. In addition to carrying over 193,000lbs of fuel 4400 miles, the KC-10A Extender will have the advantage of being able to carry cargo at the same time.

A third category of planes that is also frequently forgotten but is growing increasingly important are those involved with electronic warfare. In the past, most public attention has

focused on the exploits of photo reconnaissance planes like the U-2 and SR-71. But since the war in Vietnam, electronic warfare aircraft have found a new place in air combat. Not only do these planes provide electronic intelligence but they have also become airborne command posts capable of protecting and directing attacking or defending groups of fighters and bombers.

The best known of the American EW aircraft is the E-3A/AWACS (Airborne Warning And Control System) known as the Sentry. These horrendously expensive aircraft – over 100 million dollars each – are converted Boeing 707s with a large radome attached to the top that rotates six times a minute. The radars are linked to sophisticated computers in the plane giving the commander the capability to look down and detect aircraft for a 200 mile radius. Thus a Sentry aircraft circling over central Germany would be able to monitor aircraft – from takeoff

Above: Cutaway artwork of the A-10 Thunderbolt showing the internally mounted GAU-8/A 30mm cannon. The gun system with its ammunition drum is bigger than many small cars.

Left: A-10s on a training flight in the United States. The maximum warload for the A-10 is 16,000 pounds.

to landing – over all of East Germany and parts of Poland and as far west as the French border. Cruising at 40,000 feet the Sentry with its crew of 17 can stay airborne for 12 hours. With the ability to monitor all air traffic, and tell whether the planes are friends or foes, an Air Force commander aboard AWACS could assemble and direct his own fighters to intercept the enemy. The Israelis used a less sophisticated smaller version of the AWACS (the E-2) in just such a way during the 1982 war in Lebanon. This Hawkeye aircraft was able to alert Israeli Air Force officers to the take off of Syrian planes as soon as they left the ground. The Israelis then sent their own F-15s and F-16s to intercept and surprise the Syrians, shooting down approximately 80 MiGs without the loss of a single Israeli plane.

The Air Force uses a family of air to air missiles similar to those in service with the Navy and Marine Corps. Perhaps the Air Force's most sophisticated missile is the AIM-9L Sidewinder, a third generation air to air missile with a four mile range that homes on the infrared exhaust of the enemy aircraft. Over 15,000 Sidewinders have been produced. Each missile is nine feet long and five inches in diameter and weighs around 190lbs. The Israelis used this missile successfully in the war with Lebanon. But the Sidewinder's greatest success came in the Falklands conflict where the British fired 27 missiles and scored 23 hits. The Sparrow AIM-7 (for Air Intercept Missile) is a radar homing missile with a range of 25 miles and is 12 feet long and carries a high explosive warhead at over Mach 3.5 speeds. The Air Force has started a development program for a new missile to replace the Sparrow. In tests the new missile has been used

in look down/shoot down attacks against low flying aircraft like cruise missiles. A replacement for the Sidewinder is also being considered.

To augment its conventional bombs and unguided rockets, the Air Force has three primary air to surface missiles for close air support. The Shrike AGM (Air to Ground Missile) has appeared in twelve versions since it first made an appearance with Air Force planes during Vietnam. Shrike is a ten foot, 400lb, Mach 2 missile that homes in on the radar signals of surface to air missile batteries and destroys the site. In an effort to avoid destruction by Shrike the North Vietnamese often turned off their radars before the missile had a chance to lock on. To counter this the Air Force developed a new High Speed Anti Radiation Missile or HARM. HARM is much faster than Shrike and can lock on to the position of the enemy radars and hold it even after the emitter has been turned off.

The AGM-65 Maverick is a more complicated missile for destroying tanks and hardened targets at ranges up to 15 miles. The pilot views the target through a television monitor in the cockpit. The missile then locks onto the image and is launched allowing the pilot to turn away and escape at a considerable distance from the target. Because of the difficulty with this electro-optical target/guidance device, Maverick is limited only to daylight attacks and those in good weather. Pilots using the system have complained about the difficulty of gaining a good 'lock on' or fix on the target with the system, although the proposed laser target designator system may help overcome these problems.

Top: E-3As of the 552nd Airborne Warning and Control Wing at Tinker AFB, Oklahoma.

Above: An AIM-7 Sparrow missile fitted on a prototype F-16.

Opposite: An F-16 with wingtip-mounted Sidewinders.

Left: The GBU-15 guided weapons system is under development to add to the Air Force's range of precision guided munitions.

# MILITARY INTERVENTION

It is rather paradoxical that although the US has been in relatively few declared wars in its history, it has been involved in quite a number of small and at least two very large military 'interventions'. Intervention ranges from the use of small amounts of covert arms aid, to full-scale military commitments involving hundreds of thousands of soldiers. Such activities have occurred because administrations in Washington have often found a need to use military power to achieve American interests without the resort to a declaration of war. Such

interventions allow the US to exercise military muscle in the pursuit of goals within the shadowy area between war and peace.

## Low Level Military Intervention and Aid

The American capability to intervene extends through various levels and various degrees, depending on the circumstances and perhaps, more importantly, on the willingness of the US government to engage in such activity. As a means to an end, intervention and covert activity may be held in favor and used extensively, as they were in the Kennedy era, or fall into disfavor and disuse as they did for a time following the war in Vietnam. Low level forms of military intervention and covert military aid are designed to further US interests by gaining influence with the host country or by helping to maintain a friendly government in power. At the lowest and most common end of the scale, the US can offer military aid by assisting the armed forces of other countries. Such activities may range from the selling, at favorable prices, to granting large amounts of military equipment. At a higher level it could also include the training of the other country's military men in the US or sending US training personnel with the equipment to the client country. In certain countries the US could establish military

The deployment of US Marines to the Lebanon in 1982 was not the Marine Corps' first experience of peacekeeping in that country. Marines were also deployed to the Lebanon in the summer of 1958. Shown, above, is a Marine tank in the streets of Beirut and, right, a platoon of Marines marching to their landing ships for evacuation on 13 August.

Previous page: Marines advance supported by LVTP-7 amphibious personnel carriers during the 1980 Bright Star joint US-Egyptian exercise in Egypt.

'advisory' missions designed to train or assist local armed forces in that country, particularly in the areas of fighting insurgents. Finally, the US may actually send specialized teams of military advisors to accompany the local country's armed forces on actual combat missions.

The US Army's Special Forces Units, known more popularly as the Green Berets, are one of the main tools the US uses in its military assistance activities. The organization was founded in 1952 as an outgrowth of commando units formed in World War II. Special Forces members are carefully selected Army officers and noncommissioned officers given intensive survival, weapons, language, parachute and underwater training. The basic unit is a 12 man team made up of two officers and ten noncommissioned men. Three teams make up a company, three companies make up a battalion, and three battalions a Special Forces Group. The US currently has three Special Forces Groups with various elements stationed in the US, Panama, and West Germany.

Special Forces teams officially have the mission of carrying out unconventional warfare behind enemy lines. The units based in Germany are probably slated to be sent behind Soviet lines in the event of an invasion of NATO to disrupt Warsaw Pact rear area and supply activities. They have played other roles in the past, however. The main postwar occupation of Special Forces units has been in counterinsurgency operations. This role became especially pronounced because of the emphasis placed on counter-guerrilla operations in the Third World by the Kennedy Administration in the early 1960s.

Low levels of US military aid and activity have been used extensively since World War II. America has exported billions of dollars worth of arms to a large number of Third World countries. Sales of aircraft, ships, tanks, or other weapons, often included sending the officers and men of the country buying the arms to the US. Since 1955, for example, over 350,000 foreign military personnel have been trained in the United States. American military advisors have also been sent to many countries around the world to train armies and sometimes to take a more active role in the country's military affairs. American military advisors, for example, were instrumental in helping to train the Bolivian commandos who eventually captured Cuban guerrilla leader Che Guevara. Currently, US military advisors stationed in El Salvador are attempting to train that country's army to resist guerrilla attacks sponsored by the communist regime in Nicaragua.

American military assistance has had a number of successes and failures since 1945. Perhaps the greatest triumph occurred in the early 1950s. After a communist government came to power in Guatemala in 1951, the US gave military aid to elements in the Guatemalan Army who eventually led a coup which toppled the Marxist regime. The greatest failure came with the Bay of Pigs disaster in 1961. American forces trained dissident Cubans in Nicaragua to invade Cuba in an attempt to overthrow the Castro dictatorship. Unfortunately, inadequate military support, plus a mistaken judgement that the people would immediately rise up and oust Castro, caused the invasion to fail completely.

Military action and assistance programs shifted away from Latin America in the early 1960s to the growing insurgencies in Southeast Asia. The US provided extensive aid to Meo tribesmen and right-wing Laotian forces in the early 1960s to counter the influence of the Communist Pathet Lao and North Vietnamese forces. According to former CIA Director William Colby, the US had a secret army of over 36,000 native Laotians fighting in Laos. Special Forces teams were especially successful in setting up counter-guerrilla Civilian Irregular De-

Left: President Kennedy in conversation with Brigadier General Yarborough, Commandant of the Special Warfare Center, in October 1961. General Yarborough wears the Special Forces' Green Beret. Special Forces units were widely employed during Kennedy's presidency.

Above: Men of the 2nd Marine Division in Santo Domingo, Dominican Republic, in 1965. The Marines were deployed in an attempt to keep a communist regime from power.

fense Units in Vietnam during the war. At one time the Green Berets were operating over 80 camps in the south with an estimated 60,000 mountain tribesmen fighting in Laos, Cambodia and South Vietnam.

In the wake of the Vietnam defeat, both Congress and the American people became much more wary of military intervention abroad. It was felt that such activity originally got the US involved in Vietnam. This backlash led to the undermining of American military efforts to help pro-Western forces take power in Angola. Rather than build an army, as it had tried in the Bay of Pigs operation, Washington instead sent money and arms to help supply two guerrilla forces, the National Union for the Total Independence of Angola, (UNITA) and the Front for the Liberation of Angola (FNLA) who opposed the Moscow backed Popular Movement for the Liberation of Angola (MPLA). This aid totalled millions of dollars worth of trucks, SAMs, mortars, small arms and thousands of rifles. At the crucial point, however, Congress refused to fund additional aid. The Soviets began a large scale reinforcement of the MPLA including not only great amounts of military equipment but also a large contingent of Cuban 'volunteers' to help the MPLA fight. The MPLA and the Cuban troops eventually established a pro-Moscow communist regime in Angola and drove back the FNLA and UNITA to rural areas where they continue to fight a guerrilla war.

## Large Scale Military Intervention

By far the most common example of US military intervention is the open large scale use of American troops to protect governments, US citizens and interests, topple unfriendly governments, or a combination of all three. Such activity by the US is far from unprecedented. Fairly large-scale US military interventions have occurred in the past 200 years, predominantly in the Western Hemisphere. The use of military intervention to expand the American borders, however, sometimes led to wars, particularly with the acquisition of Texas and California. Mexico and Cuba were subjected to repeated US

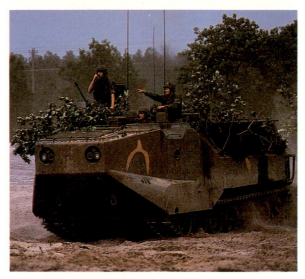

Opposite, main picture: A team from the 20th Special Forces Group seen undergoing counterinsurgency training in the Special Forces' heyday during the Kennedy years.

Both inset: Special Forces men in training for their contemporary mission of operations behind enemy lines, suitably camouflaged for prevailing weather conditions. The upper picture was taken in Puerto Rico in 1981; the lower during exercise Jack Frost 79.

Left: The LVTP-7 is the Marines' standard Amphibious Assault Vehicle. It is lightly armored and can carry 25 troops in addition to the crew of three. Road speed is almost 40mph and in the water 7.5 knots can be attained.

Below: A Marine AH-1T Sea Cobra gunship. The AH-1T is in many respects similar to the Army's AH-1S. The example shown is, however, armed with a Sidewinder missile, an arrangement the Marines are developing to give the Cobra an anti-helicopter capability.

Above: Equipment is loaded on a CH-53 Sea Stallion transport helicopter aboard the assault ship USS *Guadalcanal*. Six Marine Corps squadrons are equipped with the Sea Stallion which can carry up to 38 troops or a maximum of some 12,500 pounds of cargo.

Right: Nine Marine squadrons fly the medium-lift CH-46 Sea Knight, a design now some 20 years old and overdue for replacement. The Sea Knight can carry 26 troops.

military intervention, short of war, throughout the 1800s and well into this century. As late as 1916 American forces under the command of General Pershing entered Mexico in a futile attempt to stop the raids of Mexican warlord Francisco 'Pancho' Villa. American interventions in Cuba became so common following the Spanish-American war that the US later forced the Cubans to adopt the Platt Amendment into the Cuban constitution giving the US the right to intervene in that island whenever Washington felt it was necessary.

American military forces prior to World War II were also active in other parts of the Caribbean. President Roosevelt helped engineer Panama's successful secession from Columbia and then sent US military and naval forces to protect the new country all in an effort to pave the way for building the Panama Canal. In the 1920s US Marines in Nicaragua conducted extensive operations to crush the Sandinista insurgency.

As American military power grew, so also did its ability to intervene in areas beyond this hemisphere, such as Asia. Admiral Perry sailed his fleet into Yedo harbor Japan, trained his guns on the city and 'invited' the Japanese to sign a trade treaty which eventually opened Japan up to the West. US troops, along with a much greater number of European and

Japanese forces, were involved in China especially around the turn of the century. Washington finally withdrew its forces from mainland China only in 1937. Hawaii became part of the US after Americans on the island staged a coup against the monarchy and later invited American troops to provide protection.

American military interventions following World War II have drawn the most attention and at times have seemed unlimited in size and scope. Some have become full-scale wars in all but name. Korea and Vietnam immediately come to mind on this side of the scale. Smaller Marine forces were involved in protecting Lebanon in 1958. Almost a quarter century later Marines would again be used, along with Italian and French troops, to try to safeguard the new Lebanese government following the turmoil created by the Israeli invasion in 1982 and the expulsion of PLO forces. A large contingent of American troops landed in the Dominican Republic in 1965 to insure that a communist dominated government did not come to power. Although many would point out that no US forces were directly involved, the massive US resupply efforts to Israel in the 1967 and 1973 wars were a form of intervention to preserve an ally in danger. On the other hand of the scale, a small force of less than 100 men was used in 1980 in an attempt to free American hostages held by Iranian revolutionaries who had seized the US Embassy in Tehran.

Some of US intervention policy has been formalized by certain famous doctrines set forth by

Left: The Amphibious Assault Ship USS *Inchon* (LPH.12) and her six sisters of the *Iwo Jima* class each carry some 30 helicopters and can accomodate over 2000 Marines.

Below: The Assault Transport USS *Spiegel Grove* (LSD.32). The landing craft operated from ships like the *Spiegel Grove* complement the helicopter assault forces because they are able to deploy heavier items of equipment.

Main picture: An RH-53D Sea Stallion mine countermeasures helicopter refuels from a Marine Corps KC-130F Hercules tanker. RH-53 helicopters have been deployed aboard amphibious assault ships since minesweeping may play a vital part in landing operations.

Left: The Amphibious Assault Ship USS *Tarawa*. The five *Tarawa* class ships can operate both helicopters and landing craft (from the dock that can be seen at the stern). A Sea Stallion helicopter can be seen in flight in the foreground.

Left: Three Marine light attack squadrons are equipped with the AV-8A Harrier. The Marines' fixed wing aircraft will normally operate from US Navy aircraft carriers or shore bases but they can also fly from amphibious assault ships.

Top: Paratroops drop from a C-130 Hercules. Paratroop forces naturally offer one of the quickest and most flexible means by which the US can intervene abroad.

Above: Men of the 82nd Airborne Division move into action immediately after landing.

Presidents since 1945. The intent of such doctrines often reflects the recent success of American arms or the extent of its power at that time. At times these doctrines have been used to warn other countries of the willingness of the US to intervene militarily. The Truman and Eisenhower doctrines outlined US interests and willingness to safeguard friendly governments in postwar Europe and the Mediterranean by warning the Soviets away from these areas. These policies were instrumental in bringing stability and some measure of peace to Greece, Turkey, and the Middle East in the late 1940s and early 1950s.

More recently, Presidents have used such doctrines to set limits on US commitments. In the anti-intervention era following Vietnam, President Nixon put forth a new doctrine to reduce US military commitments abroad, especially in the context of internal insurgencies. Earlier treaties and alliances were too all encompassing and obligated the US to send in troops to suppress what might turn out not to be communist inspired and supported guerrillas but revolutionaries seeking to overthrow a cruel dictatorship. The Nixon Doctrine informed America's allies that while the US would help with material aid, it would be much more reluctant to make the commitment open ended or especially to commit American soldiers to the conflict.

## The US Marine Corps

The troops used most often by Washington for large scale interventions have been the US

Marines. Although the Marines have played a large part in all of America's declared wars, their use in undeclared conflicts has made the term 'Marines' almost synonymous with American peacetime military intervention.

As America's oldest military service, founded in 1775, the Marines have played a unique part in America's interventions for two reasons. First, before the advent of air power, the primary means of transporting large forces to distant areas, like Central America as well as Asia, was by sea. As part of the Navy, the Marines gradually developed the capability for amphibious assault operations. Second, especially since World War II, the Marines have developed into a small but complete armed force. They already had naval transport and later acquired extensive airpower, including fixed wing fighter/bomber aircraft and helicopters, outside the control of the regular Army and Air Force. Thus in a conflict smaller than World War II, Korea or Vietnam, the Marines provided all that was necessary for intervention.

At least as important, however, the Marines became the closest thing to a professional army that the United States has ever had. The Corps suffered in the post World War II era from the storms of periodic budget cutbacks and administration and public disenchantment with the military. There have been occasional attempts to disband the Corps and put it in the regular Army. Through it all, however, the Marines have maintained a high degree of *esprit de corps* in addition to being better trained and motivated than regular US Army troops. The 'can do' attitude of the Marines along with their amphibious and air capability makes them the first choice of Presidents when military intervention

Above and left: Preparing helicopters for shipment overseas. Any large-scale deployment will involve much careful preparation and considerable shipping space. Rehearsals of the reinforcement of Germany and for dealing with other contingencies are often held.

Below: Landing craft carry Marines ashore to Vieques Island, Puerto Rico, during exercise Ocean Venture 82. Exercises held near troubled areas may deter unfriendly action and make active intervention unnecessary.

is needed.

For all their famous, or infamous, reputation, the US Marine Corps has always been quite small compared to other services. Its size is often obscured by its incorporation in the Navy Department. At the present time the Corps numbers under 200,000 men and women. By an Act of Congress the Marines are ordered to maintain three divisions and three air wings. In addition to these forces they also have one re-serve division and one reserve air wing. Over 160,000 Marines are stationed in the US, 25,000 are stationed abroad (where among other duties they guard US embassies and missions), while around 5000 are on board various ships with the US fleets. Marine aircraft strength includes 450 fixed wing aircraft (F-4s, A-6s, and Harrier V/STOL aircraft) and 370 attack and transport helicopters.

Marine units reflect the necessary but in

Newly deployed troops can be supplied from the air as soon as they are established ashore. The LAPES (Low Altitude Parachute Extraction System) method shown here is very accurate and fast, ensuring that supplies land exactly where they are wanted, but may be hazardous both for the low-flying aircraft and for ground personnel.

some ways contradictory aspects of the missions that the Corps is ordered to undertake. On one hand they must be prepared for quick intervention in almost any part of the world but their missions are sometimes stretched beyond what their equipment and weapons can be expected to deal with. At 18,000 men Marine divisions are a similar size to their Army counterparts. However, because of the need to be airmobile and the limited space aboard ships, the Marines are predominantly equipped with light equipment. At the regimental level and below Marine units are armed with mortars, antitank rockets and air defense weapons such as the man-portable Stinger rocket. Other units, with heavier weapons or transport, are added according to the needs of the task to be accomplished. Marine divisions are often broken up into smaller, task-organized units based predominantly on infantry to achieve limited goals which require a quick response in a distant area.

Critics have warned that this light infantry role of Marine units, tailored primarily to assaults and interventions, could cause serious problems in the future. While a Marine unit, augmented with extra tanks and artillery in addition to its air and seaborne firepower, is more than equal to the task of invading a small island or a Third World country, it clearly is not up to the requirement of fighting a Warsaw Pact sized or armed enemy. The Marines currently have no role in a NATO defense of Europe. It is doubtful that a lightly armed Marine division could hold back or defeat a Soviet motorized rifle division that has one third less men but is based heavily on tanks and armored vehicles. While this fact is evident from looking at the equipment given to an average Marine and Soviet division, it has not stopped certain supporters from earmarking light Marine units as the primary force to stop a Soviet attack.

**The Rapid Deployment Force**

Perhaps the ultimate in US interventionary forces was set forth when President Carter authorized the establishment in 1979 of what eventually came to be known as the Rapid Deployment Force. The development of this organization was in large part the result of a need to be able to protect US interests halfway around the globe in the key oil producing regions of the Persian Gulf. After the fall of the Shah it was clear that Iran would no longer act as a bulwark against possible Soviet military expansionism. On paper the RDF was to be composed of around 200,000 men in four Army divisions and one Marine division. Using the facilities at the new base on Diego Garcia island in the Indian Ocean, the RDF (flying or sailing from the US mainland) would, in times of crisis, pick up its pre-positioned equipment and respond to the Soviet advance by landing in Iran or in another of the Persian Gulf states. From the beginning, the emphasis in the RDF was placed on being

A prototype AV-8B Advanced Harrier seen during testing. The Harrier II has been one of the most controversial items in recent defense budgets. Nonetheless, it offers considerable performance improvements over the AV-8A and the Marines intend to use it to replace both their A-4 Skyhawks and AV-8As, beginning in 1985.

able to respond quickly to a distant threat.

While the RDF was put forward by many as a force capable of stopping Soviet aggression, opponents contend it is highly unlikely that it would actually be able to do so. Recent joint exercises held between Egyptian and US forces have undoubtedly strengthened US prestige with pro-Western Arab states in the area and have made the RDF somewhat more credible to America's new Middle East allies. Critics say that in a real war, however, the Soviets have all the advantages of superior manpower, equipment and supply lines. They say that a Soviet air attack on Diego Garcia, for example, would probably destroy all the equipment stored there and end any hope that the RDF could save the Gulf. The Marine division, which would be the first US unit on the scene, would be hard pressed to stop superior Soviet forces from advancing. Although four other Army divisions are slated to reinforce the Marines later on, experts point out that these units are also allocated to reinforce NATO. If the Soviets invaded the Persian Gulf and Iran, it is more than likely that a war in Europe would already have broken out and those four divisions would be sent to hold the line in Germany, not in Kuwait.

**A Future for US Military Interventions**

The balance sheet of American postwar interventions shows that, at best, the US has had only mixed success in the use of covert and large

Military intervention in recent years has usually taken the form of peacekeeping efforts. Here men serving with the Sinai peacekeeping force assemble for an inspection. The Israeli withdrawal from Sinai was a result of the Camp David agreement which President Carter helped negotiate and the peacekeeping force helped ensure that the withdrawal was relatively trouble-free and carried out according to the agreed timetable.

Joint exercises and the provision of military training and equipment for friendly nations are among the less controversial forms of foreign intervention. Shown above is a US camp near Cairo during the 1980 Bright Star exercise. At right American and Egyptian soldiers examine a Soviet-made machine gun. The opportunity of examining the equipment of former Soviet friends is obviously welcome.

Opposite: Marines move forward mounted on a self-propelled howitzer during the Bright Star exercise.

scale military activity, short of war, to achieve its goals. On one hand American action 'saved' regimes in Guatemala, the Dominican Republic, and halted an outright invasion of Korea. On the other, intervention and covert actions in Latin America have not yielded favorable results and the large scale military intervention in Vietnam did not save that country from eventually falling to the North Vietnamese.

Despite such mixed results, it is highly likely that some degree of military intervention, whether military assistance or the deployment of US troops, will continue and may even increase in the future. While such interventions have not always proven successful or particularly attractive in the past, they often are the only means the US has. Such activity will continue because while the US does not want to acquiesce in many disturbances, threats and changes in the Third World, neither does it want to resort to full scale declared war.

Far from being hidden, the battle lines of future intervention are perhaps already being drawn. American advisors are now openly involved in training and aiding El Salvadoran government forces to resist subversion from guerrillas. President Reagan has allocated more money to expand and improve the Special

Forces – a portent that the Green Berets may soon become active around the world once again. Finally, although the Marine contingent sent to Beirut is only supposed to be involved for a limited time, it is unclear how long it will take before that force is withdrawn. Moreover, once the precedent is set to use US troops to keep the peace by keeping the two warring sides apart, they may become a necessity with any withdrawal the cause for renewed fighting.

Main picture: Marines of the 32nd Amphibious Brigade line up ready to withdraw from Beirut in November 1982.

Bottom left: LVTP-7s of the 24th Marines come ashore from ships of the Sixth Fleet to relieve the men of the 32nd Brigade being withdrawn. The peacekeeping mission in Beirut has been particularly difficult.

# BLOOD AND TREASURE

Near the end of each fiscal year, but often throughout the entire 12 months, Congress and the President assault Americans with a seemingly endless battle over the coming year's federal budget. At the center of the controversy is the size and composition of the military slice of the tax pie. How many billions of dollars more is the military getting this year than it did in the last? A favorite technique of critics is to single out specific weapons and draw unfair comparisons, citing for example that the US could purchase x number of schools or hospitals for the price of one bomber. The American public is led to believe that money for defense is merely more dollars down an endless rat hole with nothing in return for the common citizen. In fact, it would be more accurate and fair to compare it to an insurance premium. No one likes paying them, but if the need should come, you are happy that you already have it and do not have to get one after the accident.

## Human and Material Costs in War

Americans usually measure the cost of defense in terms of dollars, yet during war another column joins the balance sheet. Not only is there a cost in treasure, but also one paid in blood. Compared to other countries, the human costs of America's wars has been small. Americans fail to realize that throughout its 200 years, the US has never suffered from the ravages of war like countries in Europe and Asia. America has escaped the destruction of the total wars unique to modern times. The last invasion of the country was in the War of 1812 when the British burned the few existing buildings in the new American capital of Washington. Americans inflicted the most destruction on the US during the Civil War when the North invaded the South. None of this, however, is comparable to

Right: A Titan 34D satellite launch vehicle on the launch pad. The 34D has been developed from the earlier Titan III which in turn was a version of the Titan strategic missile – an example of how old designs can be adapted for new roles with consequent savings. Many of the satellites launched by the 34D will have military missions.

Right: The nuclear powered cruiser *Arkansas* on her trials in 1980. With two missile launchers and two gun turrets she looks under-armed when compared to Soviet contemporaries but much of her $200 million price tag goes to providing sophisticated electronics and the nuclear power needed to work with a nuclear carrier.

Previous page: An AH-64 Apache attack helicopter armed with Hellfire missiles. The Army wants to procure almost 450 Apaches but at a cost approaching $10 million apiece Congress may decline to finance the whole program.

the losses suffered by Japan, Germany, Britain, China and the USSR during World War II.

The dollar price of American wars has also been relatively cheap even though inflation tends to hide the true price of conflicts as the dollar buys less and less. The US spent only an estimated 100 million dollars to gain its freedom from Britain and 73 million to fight the Mexican War. The North spent 3.2 billion to return the secessionist states to the Union. World War II was the most expensive conflict with the price of 288 billion. Vietnam comes in a poor second at 110 billion. In all the US spent a total of about 482 billion dollars (in constant prices) for all its wars – about the cost of one defense budget in the late 1980s.

Although there really is no way to assess the cost in terms of human lives lost in war, here too the US has suffered relatively little compared to other countries. The Civil War was the most deadly conflict for the US – because Americans fought Americans – with the North losing at least 360,000 dead and the South probably as many. The US lost 405,000 men in World War II. The Soviet Union suffered an estimated 20 to 30 million civilian and military dead. The number of American civilian casualties between 1941 and 1945 was minor while a much smaller country, Poland, lost 20 percent – over six million people – of its prewar civilian population. Since the Civil War, the US casualties (killed and wounded) probably totalled between one

and one and a half million. This is roughly the loss suffered by the German military in killed, wounded, and captured during the first year after the 1941 invasion of the USSR.

**The Price of Peace**
The truly great costs of defense have come for the US during peacetime, especially in the years following World War II. Between 1791 and 1980 the total US defense bill, including wars, totalled around 2.753 trillion dollars. However, only 1.8 percent of this, around 50 billion dollars, was spent prior to 1941. The rest of the 2.710 trillion, give or take a billion, came after Pearl Harbor. The first billion dollar defense budget came only in the last year of the Civil War when the Union spent 1.3 billion dollars. American defense budgets did not reach

the billion dollar mark again until 1917, when the US became involved in another major war. In 1791 Congress authorized a total of 643,000 dollars for the Army and the Navy. In 1982 it will probably authorize a defense budget of around 228 billion. Total world defense expenditures for 1982 are around 550 billion or about 1 million dollars for each minute of the year.

Despite the efforts of Presidents Truman and Eisenhower, US defense budgets began to in-

Above: The turret of an Abrams tank under construction. Production of the Abrams has been long delayed by technical and other problems with inevitable escalation of costs.

Second left: An Abrams at high speed during trials. Despite their considerable size modern tanks are generally remarkably agile.

Left: The commander of an M60 tank traverses the turret. Western made tanks are believed to have better internal design than Soviet vehicles, allowing the crew to function more efficiently during a long engagement.

The nuclear powered attack submarine USS *Phoenix* (SSN.702) is launched from General Dynamics' Groton yard. To the right are three of the *Ohio* class Trident submarines under construction. The *Ohio*, farthest to the right, is already in the water. Irrespective of financial considerations, the production rate of nuclear submarines is low because of their complexity and because only two shipyards in the US have the necessary experience and equipment.

Right: The commander of the missile submarine *Ulysses S. Grant* at the periscope. Ballistic missile submarines have two crews to ensure that the boats spend the maximum time at sea contributing to the deterrent. While one crew is at sea with the submarine the other will be receiving shore training or be on leave.

Below: A technician installs an AN/ALQ-44 infrared jammer on a UH-1 helicopter. The jammer is designed to confuse heat-seeking missiles and increase the chance of the helicopter surviving in a hostile environment. Of course, such protection is expensive.

Above right: A soldier tries out a set of night vision goggles, useful perhaps for sentries. Other night vision devices include special sights for rifles and other weapons.

crease quickly after World War II largely as a result of the growing American military commitments around the world. The budget fell from 14 billion in 1947 to around 9 billion in 1950 but rose to 27 billion in 1952 because of the Korean War. During most of the 1950s they slowly crept up through the 30 to 40 billion dollar range and then rose steeply with the Kennedy increases in the early 1960s to reach 50 billion by 1965. Expenditures for the war in Vietnam pushed the budget to a record high of 79 billion in 1969 but the effects of inflation began to be felt as the defense dollar bought less and less.

Defense budget expenditures dropped during the early and mid 1970s in response to the anti-military feeling in the country following the Vietnam debacle. The military sector suffered doubly because not only did it receive less money but the money it did get bought very much less. By other measures the percentage of the budget and GNP devoted to defense also dropped since Vietnam. In 1968, for example, defense accounted for 42 percent of the budget

and 8 percent of the GNP. By 1975 it dropped to 26 percent of the budget and 5.8 percent of the GNP. Even with the increases projected for the 1982 budget, defense will still account for only 25 percent of the Federal budget. At 228 billion the 1982 Defense Budget is actually the first one that even approaches what the US spent in real terms on defense in 1968.

When listening to the debate on the budget most Americans form the mistaken impression that the bulk of the billions spent go to expensive strategic programs connected in one way or another to the Triad. In fact, in the new military budget the US will spend only around 17.2 billion dollars or 7.5 percent of the budget on strategic weapons programs like the Trident submarine and the MX missile. Research and development, medical care, and training account for about 18 percent more. America spends the greatest share of the defense dollar on feeding, clothing, housing, and paying the military servicemen and civilian employees of the Department of Defense. Over 93 billion dollars – 41 percent of the budget – goes toward

these 'manpower costs'. The steady growth in the cost of the general purpose, non-nuclear forces (which includes the largest amount of manpower) compared to strategic costs are evident in the fact that ten years ago general purpose forces accounted for only 33 percent of the budget costs while strategic programs took up 9.3 percent.

The advent of the volunteer army accounts for much of the increasing human costs. Now that the government has to compete with private industry for increasingly skilled talent, it must pay a comparable wage or settle for less intelligent and initially skilled personnel. Yet for all the increasing amount of money the US spends on personnel, it still has the same number of divisions (16) in 1982 that it had in 1964. The Navy will receive more money but the number of major US ships declined from 721 to 443 in the same period. Overall, the number of active duty servicemen fell from 2.6 million in 1964 to 2.1 million today.

The increases in money for men and new equipment should give qualitatively better if not quantitatively larger armed forces. There is some reason to question this hope however. Weapons are growing increasingly more expensive; more than the improvements in quality would seem to justify according to many critics of defense spending. A *Nimitz* class nuclear aircraft carrier, at over 2.2 billion dollars, costs two and one half times what a *Midway* class carrier cost in 1945. An Abrams main battle tank at two million costs 30 times what a Sherman tank cost in 1945. The price of a Polaris missile-firing nuclear submarine was 50 million dollars in the 1950s, but its replacement Trident submarine will cost over 1.8 billion in the 1980s. Naturally, inflation causes all prices to rise over time. The tanks, aircraft carriers and submarines of tomorrow will certainly be qualitatively superior to those of the past. But despite these improvements, the new costs are still hard to swallow especially when one realizes that the real cost of a black and white television today is only five percent of what it was in 1950.

New technology provides new weaponry, but not all of these new systems are expensive. Some, in fact, are so cheap relative to the systems they destroy that many military specialists believe that these weapons will revolutionize warfare. A Tomahawk cruise missile launched from a submarine costs less than a million dollars yet has the capability of sinking a Soviet cruiser or helicopter carrier worth hundreds of million of rubles. A 95,000 dollar man-portable Stinger antiaircraft missile can destroy a fighter-bomber valued at around 20 million dollars. Tanks worth over two million dollars each can fall prey to a 9000 dollar tube launched wire guided missile.

### The Life Cycle of a Weapon

Most Americans are unaware of the life cycle of a weapon system and so do not really understand where the true costs of a weapon come from or why weapons that are never built or deployed still are very expensive. The life cycle of a weapon can be very short – it may never get off the drawing board, but in the case of the B-52 bomber, that venerable workhorse of the Strategic Air Command, they also can be designed and enter service before the men who are flying them today were born.

A weapon will usually pass through five general stages during its lifetime with US forces. In the first or conceptual planning stage, military men identify an operational need for a

A picture of an OH-58 helicopter, retouched to show the proposed configuration of the design when the current Army Helicopter Improvement Program (AHIP) has been applied. The equipment above the rotor will contain infrared and TV cameras as well as a laser rangefinder and designator for Hellfire missiles. The AHIP aircraft has been designed to scout for the AH-64 attack helicopter.

new system, resulting in a prospective weapon plan/requirement that should meet defense needs. Say, for example, the Soviets are building a new super tank, with 'impenetrable' armor, and plan to deploy it in the early 1990s. The US needs a new antitank weapon capable of engaging the tank at longer range and destroying it on the first attempt. The result is a conceptual plan for a new antitank guided missile or man-portable armor piercing laser weapons.

In the second or validation stage, contractors and defense planners assess the technology and economic factors of the program in the context of current research and development to determine if such a weapon can be produced. In short, can the US produce such a weapon by the time we need it or will new areas of technology or even basic research be necessary to build the weapon? Most ideas for new weapons die somewhere in the first or second stage. No matter how great the need or desire for a new missile, technology may not be adequate to make it. The necessary research and development for the system may be so far into the realm of speculation that no firm assurances of its success can be given. More importantly, the new weapon may be more expensive to build and buy than the weapon it is designed to destroy. In such cases, planners go back to the conceptual stage to find a new weapon.

Some weapons have been amazingly adept at escaping the axe of cancellation in the validation stage and the government continues to spend money on the projects far too long. In the 1950s the US feared that it was about to fall behind the Soviets in bombers. To avoid a 'bomber gap' the US devoted billions of dollars to research and development in a futile effort to develop a nuclear powered aircraft. On the

Above: A UH-60 Black
Hawk in flight over the
Egyptian desert during the
US-Egyptian Bright Star
exercise in November 1980.
The earlier Huey transport
helicopters were more
vulnerable to ground fire as
well as having a less
satisfactory performance,
particularly in very hot
weather.

Left: An A-7 Corsair moves
in to refuel from a KC-135 of
an Air National Guard
squadron. One aspect of
recent defense budget
increases has been the
provision of up-to-date
equipment for the reserve
forces, rather than the worn
out hand-me-downs often
allocated in the past.

Opposite: A Sergeant York
gun carrier demonstrates
the mobility which it will
bring to divisional air
defense systems. The first of
these weapons will be
deployed in the mid 1980s.

Above: This NKC-135 aircraft has been used to test an airborne laser beam weapon. Early in 1983 President Reagan announced that research in laser and particle beam weapons would be stepped up with a view to developing an anti-missile system.

Right: A soldier aims a laser designator during testing of the Copperhead guided shell. The 155mm Copperhead shells are now in production and are so accurate that they can hit a moving tank at a distance of 10 miles. Although the operational advantages of such a system are self-evident, such sophisticated ammunition is so expensive that simulators may be necessary to keep training costs acceptably low.

other hand Washington killed its ICBM program in the late 1940s because of budget constraints and the judgement that technology had not progressed sufficiently to provide the engines and guidance system to make an intercontinental missile. Within a few years, however, aerospace technology advanced significantly. The Pentagon restarted missile development in the mid 1950s, leading to the successful Atlas ICBM.

The amount of time a project remains in the first two stages, before actual serial production begins, varies depending in large part on how much technology is already 'on-the-shelf' and how much completely new technology is needed

to meet the requirements. Although a highly complicated and revolutionary idea in the late 1950s, Polaris missile firing submarines borrowed much of their technology from existing nuclear submarines and solid fuel rocket technology. A working submarine was produced in only a few years. The MX missile draws extensively from existing ICBM technology, but its concept and validation phases have lasted over ten years. The US has not even test fired the new ICBM. Naturally, the longer the system remains in the first and especially second stages, the more costs increase.

A long incubation period in the validation stage also runs the risk that when the weapon finally reaches the soldier, it will be obsolete. The concept stage should take into account possible advances both in technology and the changing needs of the future battlefield. Effective crystal ball gazing is, however, exceedingly difficult. It is impossible to expect a weapons designer to be able to predict ten years in advance what technology will be available especially in electronics. Scientists cannot foresee all the possible avenues that weapons technology may follow. This gives rise to the fear that a weapon thought to be impossible or not thought of at all will suddenly appear among the enemy's forces. Both the US and the Soviets want to avoid being surprised by a new weapon on the other side. As a result, both sides allocate a great deal of research and development money to areas which never produce a weapon, but which nevertheless must be explored to avoid some technological 'Pearl Harbor'.

Once the weapon clears the concept and validation stages it then enters the production stage. During the production stage contractors produce and send at least one and usually three or four test prototypes to the Department of

Defense for approval. Although most weapons must fulfill the performance requirements stipulated by the DOD in its original concept, the Pentagon accepts some weapon systems even though they fall short because of a pressing need or because the difficulty is in a 'minor' area. Even with 1000s of hours of testing, however, problems appear after the systems enter full scale production. Both the C-5A cargo plane and the F-111 fighter bomber experienced significant problems that only became apparent

Above: A Copperhead shell demonstrates its accuracy.

Above:
A Copperhead shell showing the fins used for terminal maneuvering.

Left: The Navy's AGM-84 Harpoon missile can be launched from ships or aircraft and uses active radar guidance to achieve the accuracy shown here.

Left: The F/A-18 Hornet is designed to operate in both fighter and strike roles replacing the Phantoms and Corsairs currently in service. Employing one type of aircraft instead of two will reduce costs and improve efficiency by reducing the variety of spares which must be produced.

after the aircraft became operational and were in the production stage.

The production stage tends to be the most expensive of all periods. The government orders a large number of the new weapons involving the expenditure of billions of dollars over a few years. In many cases costs rise even more because during deployment of a weapon new basing and maintenance facilities may also have to be built. In the case of Minuteman this involved over 1000 hardened concrete silos and command centers at five Air Force bases across the United States. To service the new fleet of Trident submarines the Navy is building an entirely new base at Bangor, Washington.

In the fourth or maintenance stage, weapon systems are no longer under serial production. Initial deployment is complete although one of the production lines may remain active for a time to replace weapons destroyed in combat or

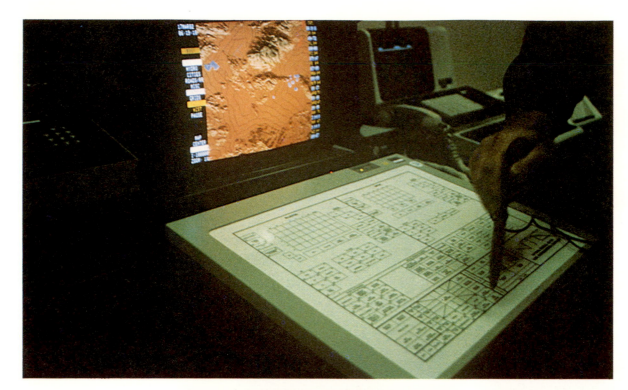

Right: Helicopter crew being trained in map reading at Fort Benning, Georgia. The board provides a realistic view of the ground and lighting and sound effects can add to the illusion. The savings in flying time are considerable.

Far right: Close up view of the pilot's HUD (head up display) in an F-16 fighter. The HUD is basically a high technology version of the traditional gunsight. Essential aircraft performance and weapons-aiming information is projected on the cockpit canopy so the pilot does not have to look down at his instruments at a critical moment.

Above: An officer sets up a tactical problem on computer training equipment. Computer and video technology can be used in many sophisticated yet cost-effective training programs by all the armed services.

Right: A soldier equipped with a receiver for signals from the Navstar Global Positioning System. This system, which should become fully operational in 1987, will enable an infantryman, ship, aircraft or other vehicle to find its exact position to an accuracy of 50 feet at the push of a button anywhere on Earth. The system will eventually use a network of 18 satellites continuously beaming signals to the ground. Because the receiving equipment is entirely passive its position will not be disclosed.

Far right: A soldier using MILES (Multiple Integrated Laser Engagement System). His M16 is fitted with a laser transmitter and his helmet and other parts of his equipment have receivers. The training value of live, moving targets who can shoot back is obvious.

accident and to provide spare parts. The maintenance stage typically is the longest period in the weapon systems life cycle. Equipment may be fitted with improvements and undergo substantial 'upgrades' to extend their useful life. All remaining B-52s have repeatedly received new electronic countermeasure or navigation devices as advanced technology became available. Some weapons like Minuteman have received new parts to such an extent that much of the missile is now substantially different from the original design. While the purchase of weapons during the production stage presents the highest lump sum costs, spending during the maintenance period for fuel, spare parts, ammunition, support facilities, and most impor-

tantly for the men to operate and service the weapons can also be quite high. Indeed, costs during the maintenance stage can be a key aspect in the initial decision to choose a weapon. A major plus in favor of Minuteman, for example, is that it costs only one quarter to maintain each year compared to a B-52 bomber.

The final stage covers the phase-out and retirement of old or obsolete weapons. While the weapons may no longer be in actual service, they still cost the taxpayer money. Merely storing equipment – such as old aircraft on desert airfields in Arizona or keeping ships mothballed in shipyards – can be expensive. A common way to end some of the costs is to sell the weapons off to foreign countries. In an age of rapidly advancing technology, however, even poor Third World countries are increasingly reluctant to buy

problems and unhappiness with a weapon after it enters the production and maintenance stage are often the result of interference or design changes made late in the validation stage. The difficulties of the Abrams battle tank graphically illustrate what happens when a design, which already has met its original specifications, must suddenly be able to meet new requirements and integrate new components. In the case of the tank, as with so many other weapons, the final result ends up failing to satisfy anyone and costing the taxpayer billions.

No matter how small the costs in human or material terms, defense never has and never will be cheap. America has been particularly fortunate in that its human casualties in war have been relatively small compared to other country's losses. When the need for world lead-

second hand weapons and insist on purchasing the most advanced, state-of-the-art weapons. Some weapons, however, can be used or later resurrected at a substantial saving. The US phased out Atlas missiles from the Triad in the early 1960s but later used them to launch satellites. Titan missiles launched all of the Gemini space capsules into orbit. During the postwar period many critics opposed the mothballing of old battleships and urged that they be sold or scrapped. The Navy brought the battleship *New Jersey* out of mothballs in the 1960s to provide valuable artillery support in the Vietnam War. The Reagan Administration wants to renovate three battleships and use them to provide seaborne fire-support for American troops in the coming decades.

Over the course of the last three decades the 'weapon acquisition process' has had its share of successes and failures. For every success like the Polaris submarine and the cruise missile, there are an equal number of Skybolt missiles and FB-111s which are failures or second rate weapons. In the end, however, humans make the decision to build or scrap a weapon. The

ership and expanded defense commitments was thrust upon the US after 1945, the country was wealthy enough to afford the costs and protect its national interest. Other countries, such as Great Britain and France, cannot afford the human or material commitments of a modern global military power and so will never attain the rank of superpower.

The question arises whether even the US will be able to afford the cost of defense in the future. Even the cost of peacetime defense has risen almost to prohibitive levels, especially when measured against many of the internal social programs the US needs which also compete for scarce tax dollars. If Americans judge that defense costs are too high, then national interests and foreign commitments probably will be reduced. Although Americans often complain about the high costs of peace, those costs may be necessary to avoid war. Indeed, in a nuclear age the costs of peace are bound to be high. But the costs of a nuclear war which begins because an enemy has judged American defenses weak after years of neglect, would be beyond comprehension in both blood and treasure.

Although the F-16, seen in production opposite, has only been in full operational use since 1980, improvements and successors are already in prospect. As well as various detailed changes to the basic F-16, major redesign efforts include the AFTI/F-16 (above) which first flew in July 1982 and the F-16XL (top left). The tail-less F-16XL may be developed for the interdiction role while the advanced flight control systems which the AFTI/F-16 is testing will be used in future generations of combat aircraft of every type.

# CHALLENGES FOR THE FUTURE

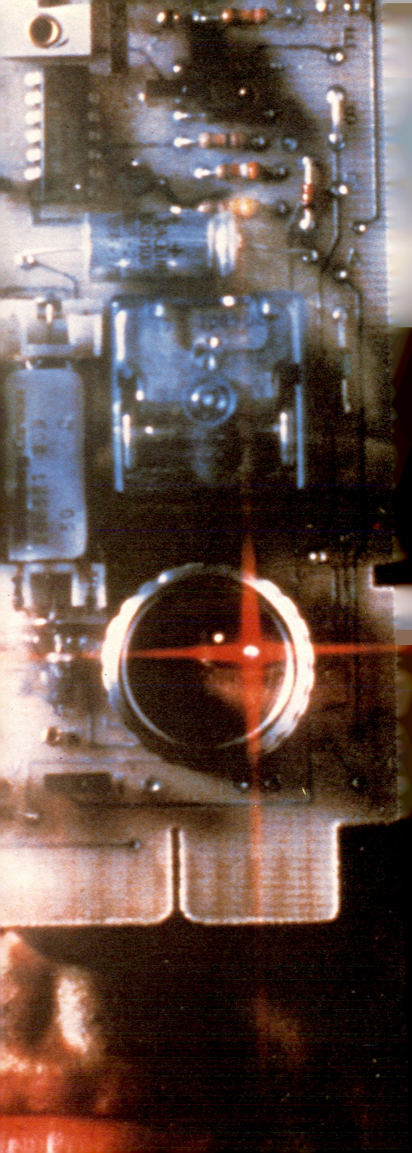

As one of the two superpowers in the world, and still the leader of the non-communist world's forces, the US will have to face and solve a continuing host of global defense problems in the future. These problems will not cover just the next two to three years but will extend over the next ten to twenty years and lead us well into the twenty-first century. They will not be limited only to changes in a particular tactic or the purchase of one weapon, but will cover the world strategic situation and America's place in it. Some of the problems are old and have been with us since 1945 and will continue to confront us. Others are just beginning to appear on the horizon and portend great changes. Washington's solutions to these defense problems will determine how the US will defend itself and its national interests, whether the US will remain a global superpower, and most basic of all, whether America will survive.

## Old Problems

Not surprisingly, questions concerning nuclear and conventional war strategy will continue to dominate the thinking of the American public and policy makers alike. American conventional war plans and capabilities will also be influenced by the potential for conflict in Europe and in many other parts of the world against non-Soviet opponents.

Above: The US armed forces, operating within a democratic alliance, must cater for many problems which presumably are less vexing within the totalitarian Warsaw Pact. Here an American tank unit commander confers with MPs and German police on a traffic problem during the Reforger exercise in September 1982.

Right: Soviet designed tanks are used in a training exercise by 'enemy' forces. Various items of Soviet-made or designed equipment have come into Western hands and have been carefully evaluated.

Previous page: A symbolic representation produced by the US Army of, according to the official caption, 'the blend of manpower and technology required to meet future challenges.'

The focus of nuclear strategy will, of course, be on the Soviet Union and Europe. Pressures from two opposing views will continue to influence American nuclear strategy and policy. On one side will be those pushing for some kind of arms limitations or reductions. Movements for arms control, banning the bomb, and a nuclear freeze have appeared periodically in the US since 1945. Because of the destructiveness of nuclear weapons such movements are very likely to continue to reappear and find a large number of concerned and genuinely well-meaning supporters among the citizenry.

Whether supporting or opposing such movements, most Americans agree that it is in the interest of the United States to maintain some form of negotiations with the Soviets on arms limitations. A chance for an agreement should never be cut off. Talks such as START and TNF should be fully explored. But as the SALT I and II talks showed, meaningful negotiations are likely to be very slow. Moreover, as both sides confront the more complicated and extremely important issues of arms reduction and verification, negotiations will become even more difficult. Finally, although both sides may be willing to enter into and continue the talks, there is no guarantee that a treaty will be signed.

The slowness of any talks and their apparent lack of progress may put the US side at a dis-advantage. Impatient, vocal, disarmament groups could put pressure on the government to reach some kind of agreement in which case the US may sacrifice key weapons or positions in haste to reach an accord. Arms control could become a key issue in future political campaigns with the danger that a candidate using the peace/disarmament issue to get elected may then be forced to deliver an agreement. Some experts have speculated that the Soviets deliberately count on this factor and delay the

talks knowing that the longer they wait the more such pressure will grow and the better the agreement that Moscow can get from the US.

Americans, especially those in the forefront of the disarmament movement will also have to accept the fact that there are limitations to what we can expect from arms negotiations. It may well be that the best treaty now possible will only result in some kind of new ceiling on new and old weapons. Even more optimistically they might bring about a small reduction in old systems or their removal from a particular area. A great reduction in the number of new and old systems is, however, unlikely. Realistically large scale reductions of nuclear arms would have to include not only the USSR and US but also the other members of the nuclear club – France, Britain, India, China – in the talks.

A Soviet observer with his escorts during a NATO exercise. Both NATO and the Warsaw Pact are careful to announce large-scale military maneuvers well in advance and permit observers so that the opposing side does not react aggressively because of fears of a surprise attack.

Meaningful results from such multi-sided talks would be hard to come by.

The other problems confronting the US nuclear policy will come from those advocating a nuclear warfighting capability and strategy. Fostered in part by the fact that the Soviets adhere to such a strategy, the idea that the US can wage and survive a nuclear war, with relatively minor casualties and damage, is again appearing with more and more support after dying out twenty years ago. Another motive behind the resurgence of warfighting among some circles undoubtedly comes from the increasing capabilities of nuclear weapons and delivery systems. In the 1960s and early 1970s, it simply was not possible to destroy the other side's deterrent in bombers, ICBMs, and missile firing submarines. Within the last five years, however, advances in weaponry have made possible the destruction, at least theoretically, of many if not all these systems.

According to proponents, the potential benefits of warfighting are great. If a true warfighting/warwinning capability could be built, not only would the country be secure but it could dictate its demands to the other side with impunity. With nuclear superiority over the Soviets, the US could supposedly deal with Moscow from an unchallengable position. The Soviets would never dare to gamble on a nuclear

war they knew beforehand they would lose. Warfighting would thus deter the Soviets.

The costs and risks of miscalculating with warfighting, however, are even greater. Most warfighting scenarios are based on a number of suspect assumptions. Advocates believe that all the enemy's nuclear weapons could be destroyed – a dangerous assumption since the survival of just a few weapons could cause great damage to the US. They also seem to forget that the Soviets are working diligently to improve their own weapon technology. The two sides' search for warfighting capabilities might end up with nothing more than a continuing vain attempt by both of them to gain something that neither can ever achieve because of the efforts of the other. At the very least, the search for a warfighting capability could result in the needless expenditure of billions of dollars and roubles. At most it could result in one side issuing an ultimatum that could force both to the brink of nuclear war and perhaps beyond.

American conventional strategy will probably remain largely defensive or reactive. Despite the movement toward an Airland ground strategy, the US is not pursuing the objective of carrying the war to the enemy first in conventional warfare. American and NATO strategy will still be to defend the alliance and not allow the other side to advance into Western Europe, the Middle East, or Asia. Such a strategy, however, leaves the initiative with the Soviets. It allows them to chose the time and place where a military challenge and pressure will be initiated. The US only has the option of responding – perhaps with too little, too late.

The defensive/reactive posture is perhaps forced on the US because of limitations in manpower and equipment for the existing commitments. The US cannot have military forces everywhere in the world where it has responsibilities and interests. But because America has global commitments – and thus an American military presence of some kind or a credible military capability is necessary in many areas of the world – the US is in the dangerous posi-

Left: A soldier in full protective clothing applies a decontaminant chemical to his rifle during training in chemical warfare precautions. The US maintains a stockpile of chemical munitions but these are very old and recent defense programs have included highly controversial plans for new designs.

Above: A CH-3E helicopter of the Air Force Reserve 302nd Special Operations Squadron on a training flight near Luke AFB, Arizona. Reserve forces play a vital part in NATO mobilisation plans but deploying men and equipment from the US in time of war will be fraught with difficulty.

Left: A mock-up of the proposed launch vehicle for ground based cruise missiles. The proposals to deploy this system to European bases have met with considerable opposition.

An EA-6B Prowler electronic warfare aircraft. Each aircraft carrier normally embarks roughly four of these aircraft, designed to accompany attack forces and jam enemy radars. Matters relating to electronic warfare are usually highly classified so assessments are difficult. Some published reports suggest, however, that this is one of the areas in which Soviet technology is most advanced.

tion of spreading its military resources too thin. It is not providing a convincing military capability in many areas.

Europe, and especially Germany, traditionally have been marked as the likeliest area of future superpower conflict in the postwar years. Ironically, some believe that war in Europe has actually become, and may well continue to grow, more and more unlikely. But the reasons for this 'stability' are not at all favorable to the United States and its security.

The US will probably never use its armed forces in Europe to aid any communist satellite struggling to escape the Bear's embrace. A

chance to take such a step came and was declined during the Hungarian crisis in 1956. The decision not to interfere in the Soviet sphere of influence (Eastern Europe) was confirmed in 1968 over Czechoslovakia and probably would have occurred again had the Soviets invaded Poland in 1982. Any real thought of 'rolling back' communism ended in the 1950s with John Foster Dulles. The Soviets can be fairly secure in their region and have no need to fear a NATO attack.

The threat of future war would seem, therefore, to be restricted to a Warsaw Pact attack on NATO. But Nato may slowly be crumbling and Moscow need not attack, some experts claim, but only wait until the alliance falls apart of its own tensions and disagreements. The alliance members are suffering a continuing and serious crisis of will, and fail to recognize and counter the military threat posed by the Warsaw Pact. This erosion of will began in the late 1960s with West Germany's Ostpolitik policy of improving relations with the Soviet Union. The feeling that the Soviet Union and the rest of the Pact countries present less and less of a threat to Western Europe has spread ever since to many parts of European society and government. Its latest expression is evident in the efforts of certain groups to block deployment of the cruise missile and Pershing II missiles along with

Main picture: The nuclear-powered, guided missile cruiser *Long Beach* was the first nuclear-powered surface warship to be built, being completed shortly before the carrier *Enterprise*. She is easily recognised by her square sided bridge structure which in fact is made up of various radar antennae.

other badly needed NATO modernization programs.

Thus with the Atlantic alliance already under strains, the Soviets are not likely to risk war in an area that may become more and more neutral and accommodating to them in the future anyway. Moscow would not risk any conflict that could result in escalation to strategic nuclear war when it is unnecessary. Although this line of thought is perhaps exaggerated, a growing lack of support for NATO among the people of Western Europe lends it a disturbing amount of credence.

**New Challenges and Panaceas**
The old problems of nuclear and conventional war have been joined by new problems which will tax American military power in the future. Although the US has dealt in some fashion with the problem of nuclear weapons proliferation, plans have never really come to grips with the prospect of a war involving any of the so called 'lesser nuclear powers.' Little thought has been given not only to what this means for American defense but also for that of our allies. In addition, while the US has been involved in conflicts only outside Europe since 1945, the American forces' capabilities to fight wars around the world need further strengthening. Both of these new problems, coupled with the ever-present spectre of rising defense costs, are likely to lead to strains on American military power.

Above: The NATO IIIB communications satellite which was launched in 1977. Communications and reconnaissance satellites may be among the first targets struck in a future world war.

Right: Weather satellite photographs are a familiar part of every TV weather forecast but accurate forecasting is so important in many military matters that the armed services maintain their own satellite system for this purpose. The illustration shows the control center for this program at Fairchild AFB, Washington.

The spectacular launch by an Atlas Centaur rocket of a US Navy communications satellite in October 1980. The Navy has its own communications system, with at least three satellites in stationary orbits over the equator at all times, to give virtually world-wide coverage.

states will necessarily present a direct nuclear threat to the US. Few of them will ever develop the means to deliver an atomic weapon over long ranges even though they may test and develop nuclear weapons. Nevertheless, they still will present a dangerous threat to US national security interests.

The nuclear proliferation threat to the US comes from the possibility that these lesser nuclear powers may use their nuclear weapons in a local conflict. Such a war could conceivably eventually involve the US and the Soviet Union with the chance of escalation to a superpower nuclear exchange. More likely, the lesser nuclear powers will use their weapons against each other or a US ally. The conflict between Iran and Iraq – both of which could presumably have nuclear weapons in the future – points out the wider implications to the US and its allies of nuclear conflict in the oil-rich areas of the Middle East. What would have happened if Argenti-

Above: Armed forces training also includes instruction in dealing with civil disturbance. Members of the Iowa National Guard are shown during a riot control exercise.

Right: The National Guard provides many support services for the front-line forces. Here National Guardsmen set up what the Army calls a MUST (Medical Self-Contained Transportable) Hospital.

The greatest prospect of future nuclear war facing American military power may not come from the Soviet Union. The Soviets will continue to be the only power capable of launching an annihilating nuclear attack on the US but they may be less likely than other states to use nuclear weapons. The rising new threat comes from the proliferation of nuclear weapons among many smaller countries.

The list of countries actively working on or believed already to have nuclear weapons grows each year. Brazil, Israel, South Africa, and South Korea to name a few could join the nuclear club within a few years. In fact, many experts believe that between ten and twenty countries may be involved, to some extent, in developing nuclear weapons or could develop them in the next ten years. Not all of these

na had threatened to use nuclear weapons against the British in the conflict over the Falkland Islands? Although Israel is often held up as an example of an 'almost' nuclear power that has refrained from testing a weapon and has never even considered using one in combat, the hope that all countries will act in such a restrained manner is in vain. The likelihood of atomic bombs being used would increase greatly if someone like Libya's General Gaddafi came into possession of the weapons. Moreover, once the firebreak or precedent on the use of nuclear weapons had been broken, their use in future military conflicts would probably become much more common.

The proliferation of nuclear weapons will make America's use of military force abroad more difficult. Although the US is unlikely to

A key item of equipment for the 1980s, the Bradley Infantry Fighting Vehicle.

face a direct military challenge in Europe, this does not mean that the need to use military force will not occur in other parts of the world. There is always a chance that American troops will become involved in wars in other parts of the globe not directly against the Soviets. Latin America will continue to experience internal insurgencies like the one in El Salvador. Warfare in the rest of South America and in Subsaharan Africa is still very much a possibility. Thus, American military forces will be needed even more in areas outside Europe.

The most likely area where American forces will fight is in the volatile Middle East. The oil glut of the early 1980s will not last forever, making the Arab oilfields vital once again. Some progress has been made toward settling the issue of a Palestinian state, but the odds are still in favor of continuing conflict. Sentiment favoring Israel has declined in the US following the Israeli invasion of Lebanon, but it is still likely that the US would send some kind of military aid or force to the Middle East if Israel was seriously threatened by some outside power or the flow of oil from the Gulf states was cut. Even if a settlement between Israel and its Arab neighbors comes about, the area is still filled with flashpoints – Egypt and Libya, Pakistan and India, or Afghanistan, Iran and Iraq – where the US could become involved. All of these potential conflicts will demand that the US has a very strong military capability to exert considerable military power quickly in areas halfway around the world.

An instructor at Fort Knox explains the characteristics of the Soviet Kalashnikov assault rifle to a group of recruits. The Kalashnikov is standard equipment throughout the Warsaw Pact.

In order to conserve its military resources, some experts have advocated that the US should attempt to delegate security responsibility by building up surrogate military powers that would insure stability in the areas. The past record of such surrogate forces, however, does not portend any great success for such a panacea. During the 1960s and into the 1970s the US sold billions of dollars of sophisticated weaponry to the Shah of Iran. Arguments in favor of these sales stated that Iranian armed forces were being built up to make Iran the defender of US interests in the Persian Gulf. But the Shah fell because of internal problems.

An F-15 Eagle in flight. Although the Eagle is, plane for plane, one of the best fighter aircraft currently in service, its critics suggest that in a large scale engagement a pilot will not be able to make full use of its capabilities and will, therefore, fall prey to simpler, more numerous Soviet opponents.

Defense Secretary Caspar Weinberger at a March 1983 press conference to announce the publication of a report on the Soviet armed forces. In the background a painting of the Soviet 'Blackjack' long-range bomber the existence of which was officially admitted for the first time in the report.

The Joint Chiefs of Staff in early 1983. From left, Admiral Watkins, USN, General Meyer, USA, General Barrow, USMC, General Vessey, USA, Chairman, and General Gabriel, USAF. The JCS organisation is designed to provide co-ordination between the three services and give the highest standards of non-partisan professional advice to the government. Critics suggest that the supporting staff for the chiefs is too small and that the members of the staff and the individual chiefs tend too often to support the views most acceptable to their parent services.

His armed forces were decimated by religious purges effectively ending the protectorship of US interests in the region. The fact that a surrogate – so carefully built up and armed over many years – could fall so quickly with the incoming government so hostile to the United States casts serious doubt on the value of surrogates in the future.

Other advocates contend, however, that much more politically stable countries are available to protect or indirectly advance important US interests in key areas of the world. They recommend that the US make a major effort to upgrade the defense capabilities of China for example. They also insist that Japan undertake a major rearmament or at least begin to assume some of the burden for the defense of the Asian region. They say a modernized Chinese army would offer a major counterweight to the Soviets and force Moscow to commit even more

of its military resources to the border areas. Rearming China, however, would be an undertaking costing tens of billions of dollars. More importantly, the US would have no control over how and against whom the Chinese would use their new strength. An American rearmament of Japan would be a cause for major alarm among the smaller countries of Southeast Asia. Any Japanese rearmament would also probably cause serious worries in Peking.

## No Easy Solutions

How then can the US use its limited military resources to deal with problems in strategy, NATO, nuclear proliferation, and ever-increasing costs all of which are linked to continuing and perhaps expanding global commitments? How can American military power defend US national interests in the future against growing pressures and threats? There are no easy, quick, or cheap answers, but there are answers.

The essence of the nuclear peace for the years to come depends on the continued maintenance of a nuclear balance. Advocates of both disarmament and warfighting underestimate the stability that the nuclear stalemate has brought to the world. It is important to remember the obvious; there have been no nuclear wars over the last forty years. Some measure of stability has been gained through the balance of terror. Although it is easy to speculate that other paths might be more politically or militarily advantageous, if none of these is realistically achieveable then the present stability is preferable to disruption and potential disaster.

Americans may have to realize that a nuclear-free world is not possible, that the US will probably always have to have some nuclear weapons, and that the main concern of our political and military leaders should perhaps be the attainment of a nuclear *safe* world. The political extremes may not like mutual assured destruction, but it does work. The US would waste billions seeking an unobtainable and destabilizing warfighting capability. On the other hand, the country as a whole must not succumb to the strident demands of certain foreign and domestic groups calling for blind acceptance of ill-considered disarmament schemes.

A key part of future American nuclear strategy should include stronger measures to attempt to limit the spread of nuclear military technology beyond the countries it has already reached. This includes not only monitoring the supply of nuclear technology to other countries but also making increased efforts to stop the movement or development of any technology that such countries could use to produce delivery systems for such weapons. Without extensive political and economic measures toward this end, the US may someday face not only the superpower of the Soviet Union, but also lesser nuclear powers with the potential to destroy American allies and draw the US into a wider

war. Taking restrictive measures at that time may be too late and will certainly be more expensive even if they are possible at all.

Because of the nature of western political systems and their decision against striking first, the NATO alliance will remain defensive in nature. This does not mean, however, that the US should refrain from efforts to try constantly to strengthen the alliance politically and militarily against the very real threat that the Soviets and the other Warsaw Pact countries present. The US should make more efforts to win the political battle in Europe and turn public opinion in favor of NATO's plans which are for Europe's defense. President Reagan's 'Zero Option' plan was a step in the right direction that puts the Soviets on the defensive on the disarmament issue in Europe. Other proposals could also put the Soviets in the position of having to deliver on their propaganda claims on disarmament.

Europe and NATO, while important, should not totally dominate American military thinking the way they have in the past. In the next twenty years the US will need to increase its military strength and capabilities in both sea

Above: An F-14 Tomcat fighter shadows a Soviet Tu-95 Bear reconnaissance aircraft on a mission near Guam. Soviet planes continually probe US and other Western defense systems and are regularly met and turned away.

Left: Two Venezuelan frigates lead the USS *Jesse L. Brown* (FF.1089) during the exercise Unitas XX in 1979, a readiness exercise involving the United States and seven South American nations.

and air transport for global efforts. The Rapid Deployment Force could well become the prototype of a combined sea-air-land assault force. In addition to transport and fighting capabilities, the US will have to reverse the trend of the last twenty years and try to increase the number of strategic foreign bases to support operations. The facilities established at Diego Garcia in the Indian Ocean represent an excellent example of a key forward base needed for long range power projection.

Clearly the US must also begin today to plan not just for war in the next five years, but to lay the groundwork for weapons and programs that will be used in the year 2000. Planning for hardware commands great attention if only because of the tremendous costs involved. The keels of the aircraft carriers being laid today will still be in active service in the next century. Rather than turn away from technology, which some see as the main cause of increasing defense costs, the US should embrace it as the way to make weapons both more effective and cheaper. Cruise missiles, smart bombs and wire guided antitank rockets, are examples of high-technology weapons that are effective and relatively cheap. The US will also have to make long term investments in the area of electronics to maintain a critical lead over its potential enemies.

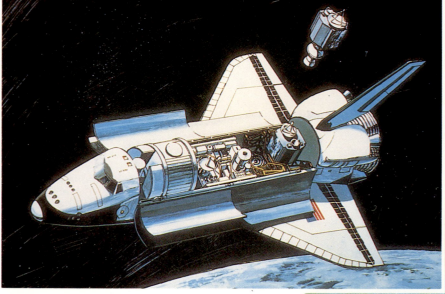

Above: Artist's impression of the Space Shuttle launching the payload assist module which is designed to boost satellites to a higher orbit than the shuttle itself is capable of attaining. Many military satellites must use such orbits.

Top right: A picture taken from the Shuttle in December 1981 of the troubled Persian Gulf. Iran is at the top of the picture and Oman at the bottom left.

Main picture: The spectacular launch of the Space Shuttle. This is the 11 November 1982 launch of *Columbia*, carrying the Shuttle's first commercial payload. More than one third of the Shuttle's missions over the next ten years will, however, be on behalf of the Department of Defense.

In planning for tomorrow's defenses the US will also have to continue to devote adequate time and money to what promises to be one of the most important areas of conflict in the future – outer space. Space warfare is, in many respects, already going on. The US Space Shuttle has carried out missions in which military payloads were put in orbit and many more military missions are scheduled. The Air Force and Army reportedly are working on anti-satellite systems and laser weapons capable of destroying aircraft or incoming warheads in flight, and enemy satellites in orbit. In the future the side that controls outer space can make his adversary deaf, dumb, and blind on the air, land or sea battle below.

The costs of all future defense endeavors will continue to go up and go up sharply in some periods. There are ways to limit defense cost increases although they will not be popular. While the price of new airplanes and some weapons can sometimes be reduced by finding cheaper yet adequate alternatives, the trend toward more expensive hardware is here to stay. Substantial savings could, however, be made by reducing manpower costs but not manpower. In order to maintain a large, well trained defense force which American commitments require, the US may have to reintroduce the unpopular but necessary step of conscription – the draft. In this way the US could, at an acceptable cost, keep in uniform the large number of men it needs and retain the trained technological specialists who will become more and more necessary for American defense as time goes on.

Finally, to make use of all the men, weapons, and equipment bases, the US will have to insure that the government and people maintain the will to use that military. This undoubtedly will be one of the hardest tasks of all. It is evident that America cannot decrease its commitments abroad and that its national interests will remain at risk – conflict and war will therefore remain a distinct possibility. The ability to deter or defeat any foes will depend on American willingness to use military force on a level which may range from military aid to a large scale commitment of troops. The ability to convince friends and foes alike that the US is willing to spend blood and treasure to protect and secure its national interests is, for the future, perhaps the most important need of US military power.

The Shuttle *Challenger* being moved from the Rockwell manufacturing site to Edwards AFB from which it will be transported by air to the launch pad at Kennedy Space Center, a picture taken in July 1982. President Reagan's 1983 announcement of accelerated research in anti-missile technology can only confirm the vital part the military uses of outer space will play in America's defense in the future.

# INDEX

# Acknowledgements

The publishers would like to thank Design 23 who designed this book and Ron Watson who compiled the index. The majority of the pictures were provided by various official US government agencies including the Public Affairs and Audiovisual Services of the Department of Defense, the US Army, the US Navy and the US Air Force in Washington DC, the Public Affairs offices of the Army and Marine Corps in New York and the Public Affairs offices of US Army DARCOM and US Army TRADOC. In addition thanks are also owed to the following agencies and individuals for the illustrations appearing on the pages indicated.

Avco Corp: p 54 upper. Michael Badrocke (artwork): pp 62-63, 146-147, 160-161. Bell Helicopter Textron: pp 84 top, 193. Black Star: p 35 lower. Boeing: pp 44-46, 45 lower, 137 lower, 138 main picture. Bowen-McLaughlin York: pp 88 top, 89 lower. British Aerospace: p 175 top. Ford Aerospace: p 175 top. FMG Corporation: p 175 top. General Dynamics: pp 56 center, 58 top, 60-61, 111 lower, 112 top, 129 right, 139 lower, 145 top, 164 lower, 200 both, 201. General Motors: p 80 top. Grumman: p 149 both. Imperial War Museum, London: p 137 top. Hughes Aircraft: pp 90 lower, 158 top. Hughes Helicopters; p 87 top. Robert Hunt Library: pp 28 lower, 33 lower. Martin Marietta: pp 55, 102 both, 105 top, 188 top, 196 lower, 197 top and center right. McDonnell Douglas: p 140 top. NASA: pp 210 top, 211, 218-219 all three, 220-221. Rockwell International: pp 86 top, 165 bottom. Ken Smith (artwork) 150-1, 162-3. Texas Instruments: p 159 lower. Vought Corporation: pp 103, 124, 151 top, 194-195. Wide World Photographs: pp 25 center and bottom, 40 all three, 168 bottom, 216 top. White House (photo by Michael Evans): p 206.